Sound and Light

interactive SCIENCE

PEARSON

Boston, Massachusetts
Chandler, Arizona
Glenview, Illinois
Upper Saddle River, New Jersey

AUTHORS

You're an author!

As you write in this science book, your answers and personal discoveries will be recorded for you to keep, making this book unique to you. That is why you are one of the primary authors of this book.

✏️ **In the space below, print your name, school, town, and state. Then write a short autobiography that includes your interests and accomplishments.**

YOUR NAME _____

SCHOOL _____

TOWN, STATE _____

AUTOBIOGRAPHY _____

_____

_____

_____

_____

_____

_____

Your Photo

Acknowledgments appear on pages 144–145, which constitute an extension of this copyright page.

ISBN-13:   978-0-13-368482-7
ISBN-10:   0-13-368482-2

6 7 8 9 10 V011 15 14 13 12

ON THE COVER
Waves in Action
Both sound and light travel from place to place in the form of waves. When the musician puckers his lips and blows into the trumpet, he creates sound waves. Reflected light waves create the image of the marching band that you see in the rim of the horn.

Program Authors

DON BUCKLEY, M.Sc.
Information and Communications Technology Director,
The School at Columbia University, New York, New York
Mr. Buckley has been at the forefront of K–12 educational technology for nearly two decades. A founder of New York City Independent School Technologists (NYCIST) and long-time chair of New York Association of Independent Schools' annual IT conference, he has taught students on two continents and created multimedia and Internet-based instructional systems for schools worldwide.

ZIPPORAH MILLER, M.A.Ed.
Associate Executive Director for Professional Programs and Conferences, National Science Teachers Association, Arlington, Virginia
Associate executive director for professional programs and conferences at NSTA, Ms. Zipporah Miller is a former K–12 science supervisor and STEM coordinator for the Prince George's County Public School District in Maryland. She is a science education consultant who has overseen curriculum development and staff training for more than 150 district science coordinators.

MICHAEL J. PADILLA, Ph.D.
Associate Dean and Director, Eugene P. Moore School of Education, Clemson University, Clemson, South Carolina
A former middle school teacher and a leader in middle school science education, Dr. Michael Padilla has served as president of the National Science Teachers Association and as a writer of the National Science Education Standards. He is professor of science education at Clemson University. As lead author of the *Science Explorer* series, Dr. Padilla has inspired the team in developing a program that promotes student inquiry and meets the needs of today's students.

KATHRYN THORNTON, Ph.D.
Professor and Associate Dean, School of Engineering and Applied Science, University of Virginia, Charlottesville, Virginia
Selected by NASA in May 1984, Dr. Kathryn Thornton is a veteran of four space flights. She has logged over 975 hours in space, including more than 21 hours of extravehicular activity. As an author on the *Scott Foresman Science* series, Dr. Thornton's enthusiasm for science has inspired teachers around the globe.

MICHAEL E. WYSESSION, Ph.D.
Associate Professor of Earth and Planetary Science, Washington University, St. Louis, Missouri
An author on more than 50 scientific publications, Dr. Wysession was awarded the prestigious Packard Foundation Fellowship and Presidential Faculty Fellowship for his research in geophysics. Dr. Wysession is an expert on Earth's inner structure and has mapped various regions of Earth using seismic tomography. He is known internationally for his work in geoscience education and outreach.

Instructional Design Author

GRANT WIGGINS, Ed.D.
President, Authentic Education, Hopewell, New Jersey
Dr. Wiggins is a co-author of the "Understanding by Design Handbook". His approach to instructional design provides teachers with a disciplined way of thinking about curriculum design, assessment, and instruction that moves teaching from covering the content to ensuring understanding.

The Association for Supervision of Curriculum Development (ASCD), publisher of the "Understanding by Design Handbook" co-authored by Grant Wiggins and registered owner of the trademark "Understanding by Design", has not authorized, approved or sponsored this work and is in no way affiliated with Pearson or its products.

Planet Diary Author

JACK HANKIN
Science/Mathematics Teacher, The Hilldale School, Daly City, California Founder, Planet Diary Web site
Mr. Hankin is the creator and writer of Planet Diary, a science current events Web site. He is passionate about bringing science news and environmental awareness into classrooms and offers numerous Planet Diary workshops at NSTA and other events to train middle and high school teachers.

ELL Consultant

JIM CUMMINS, Ph.D.
Professor and Canada Research Chair, Curriculum, Teaching and Learning department at the University of Toronto
Dr. Cummins focuses on literacy development in multilingual schools and the role of technology in promoting student learning across the curriculum. *Interactive Science* incorporates essential research-based principles for integrating language with the teaching of academic content based on his instructional framework.

Reading Consultant

HARVEY DANIELS, Ph.D.
Professor of Secondary Education, University of New Mexico, Albuquerque, New Mexico
Dr. Daniels is an international consultant to schools, districts, and educational agencies. He has authored or coauthored 13 books on language, literacy, and education. His most recent works are *Comprehension and Collaboration: Inquiry Circles in Action* and *Subjects Matter: Every Teacher's Guide to Content-Area Reading.*

REVIEWERS

Contributing Writers

Edward Aguado, Ph.D.
Professor, Department of Geography
San Diego State University
San Diego, California

Elizabeth Coolidge-Stolz, M.D.
Medical Writer
North Reading, Massachusetts

Donald L. Cronkite, Ph.D.
Professor of Biology
Hope College
Holland, Michigan

Jan Jenner, Ph.D.
Science Writer
Talladega, Alabama

Linda Cronin Jones, Ph.D.
Associate Professor of Science and Environmental Education
University of Florida
Gainesville, Florida

T. Griffith Jones, Ph.D.
Clinical Associate Professor of Science Education
College of Education
University of Florida
Gainesville, Florida

Andrew C. Kemp, Ph.D.
Teacher
Jefferson County Public Schools
Louisville, Kentucky

Matthew Stoneking, Ph.D.
Associate Professor of Physics
Lawrence University
Appleton, Wisconsin

R. Bruce Ward, Ed.D.
Senior Research Associate
Science Education Department
Harvard-Smithsonian Center for Astrophysics
Cambridge, Massachusetts

Content Reviewers

Paul D. Beale, Ph.D.
Department of Physics
University of Colorado at Boulder
Boulder, Colorado

Jeff R. Bodart, Ph.D.
Professor of Physical Sciences
Chipola College
Marianna, Florida

Joy Branlund, Ph.D.
Department of Earth Science
Southwestern Illinois College
Granite City, Illinois

Marguerite Brickman, Ph.D.
Division of Biological Sciences
University of Georgia
Athens, Georgia

Bonnie J. Brunkhorst, Ph.D.
Science Education and Geological Sciences
California State University
San Bernardino, California

Michael Castellani, Ph.D.
Department of Chemistry
Marshall University
Huntington, West Virginia

Charles C. Curtis, Ph.D.
Research Associate Professor of Physics
University of Arizona
Tucson, Arizona

Diane I. Doser, Ph.D.
Department of Geological Sciences
University of Texas
El Paso, Texas

Rick Duhrkopf, Ph.D.
Department of Biology
Baylor University
Waco, Texas

Alice K. Hankla, Ph.D.
The Galloway School
Atlanta, Georgia

Mark Henriksen, Ph.D.
Physics Department
University of Maryland
Baltimore, Maryland

Chad Hershock, Ph.D.
Center for Research on Learning and Teaching
University of Michigan
Ann Arbor, Michigan

Jeremiah N. Jarrett, Ph.D.
Department of Biology
Central Connecticut State University
New Britain, Connecticut

Scott L. Kight, Ph.D.
Department of Biology
Montclair State University
Montclair, New Jersey

Jennifer O. Liang, Ph.D.
Department of Biology
University of Minnesota–Duluth
Duluth, Minnesota

Candace Lutzow-Felling, Ph.D.
Director of Education
The State Arboretum of Virginia
University of Virginia
Boyce, Virginia

Cortney V. Martin, Ph.D.
Virginia Polytechnic Institute
Blacksburg, Virginia

Joseph F. McCullough, Ph.D.
Physics Program Chair
Cabrillo College
Aptos, California

Heather Mernitz, Ph.D.
Department of Physical Science
Alverno College
Milwaukee, Wisconsin

Sadredin C. Moosavi, Ph.D.
Department of Earth and Environmental Sciences
Tulane University
New Orleans, Louisiana

David L. Reid, Ph.D.
Department of Biology
Blackburn College
Carlinville, Illinois

Scott M. Rochette, Ph.D.
Department of the Earth Sciences
SUNY College at Brockport
Brockport, New York

Karyn L. Rogers, Ph.D.
Department of Geological Sciences
University of Missouri
Columbia, Missouri

Laurence Rosenhein, Ph.D.
Department of Chemistry
Indiana State University
Terre Haute, Indiana

Sara Seager, Ph.D.
Department of Planetary Sciences and Physics
Massachusetts Institute of Technology
Cambridge, Massachusetts

Tom Shoberg, Ph.D.
Missouri University of Science and Technology
Rolla, Missouri

Patricia Simmons, Ph.D.
North Carolina State University
Raleigh, North Carolina

William H. Steinecker, Ph.D.
Research Scholar
Miami University
Oxford, Ohio

Paul R. Stoddard, Ph.D.
Department of Geology and Environmental Geosciences
Northern Illinois University
DeKalb, Illinois

John R. Villarreal, Ph.D.
Department of Chemistry
The University of Texas–Pan American
Edinburg, Texas

John R. Wagner, Ph.D.
Department of Geology
Clemson University
Clemson, South Carolina

Jerry Waldvogel, Ph.D.
Department of Biological Sciences
Clemson University
Clemson, South Carolina

Donna L. Witter, Ph.D.
Department of Geology
Kent State University
Kent, Ohio

Edward J. Zalisko, Ph.D.
Department of Biology
Blackburn College
Carlinville, Illinois

Museum of Science.

Special thanks to the Museum of Science, Boston, Massachusetts, and Ioannis Miaoulis, the Museum's president and director, for serving as content advisors for the technology and design strand in this program.

CONTENTS

Lab zone® Enter the Lab zone for hands-on inquiry.

Chapter Lab Investigation:
• Directed Inquiry: Making Waves
• Open Inquiry: Making Waves

Inquiry Warm-Ups: • What Are Waves?
• What Do Waves Look Like? • How Does a Ball Bounce?

Quick Labs: • What Causes Mechanical Waves? • Three Types of Waves • Properties of Waves • What Affects the Speed of a Wave? • Wave Interference • Standing Waves

my science online.com

Go to MyScienceOnline.com to interact with this chapter's content.
Keyword: Characteristics of Waves

> UNTAMED SCIENCE
• Extreme Wave Science!

> PLANET DIARY
• Characteristics of Waves

> INTERACTIVE ART
• Wave Interference • Properties of Waves

> ART IN MOTION
• Wave and Energy Movement

> VIRTUAL LAB
• Bouncing and Bending Light

CHAPTER 2

Sound

 Lab zone® Enter the Lab zone for hands-on inquiry.

Chapter Lab Investigation:
• Directed Inquiry: Changing Pitch
• Open Inquiry: Changing Pitch

Inquiry Warm-Ups: • What Is Sound?
• How Does Amplitude Affect Loudness?
• What Is Music? • Hearing Sound • How Can You Use Time to Measure Distance?

Quick Labs: • Understanding Sound
• Ear to the Sound • Listen to This • Pipe Sounds • How Can You Change Pitch?
• Design and Build Hearing Protectors
• Designing Experiments

my science online.com

Go to MyScienceOnline.com to interact with this chapter's content.
Keyword: Sound

> UNTAMED SCIENCE
• Was That a Whale I Heard?

> PLANET DIARY
• Sound

> INTERACTIVE ART
• Musical Instruments • Exploring Sound Waves

> ART IN MOTION
• Observing the Doppler Effect

> REAL-WORLD INQUIRY
• How Can Sound Solve a Problem?

CONTENTS

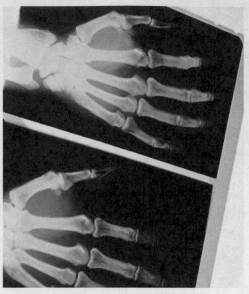

Lab zone — **Enter the Lab zone for hands-on inquiry.**

Chapter Lab Investigation:
• Directed Inquiry: Build a Crystal Radio
• Open Inquiry: Build a Crystal Radio

Inquiry Warm-Ups: • How Fast Are
Electromagnetic Waves? • What Is White
Light? • How Can Waves Change?

Quick Labs: • What Is an Electromagnetic
Wave Made Of? • Waves or Particles?
• Differences Between Waves • Parts of the
Electromagnetic Spectrum • How Cell Phones
Work • How Does GPS Work?

my science online.com

**Go to MyScienceOnline.com to
interact with this chapter's content.
Keyword: Electromagnetic Waves**

> UNTAMED SCIENCE
• The Day the Waves Died

> PLANET DIARY
• Electromagnetic Waves

> INTERACTIVE ART
• Electromagnetic Waves • Modulating
Electromagnetic Waves

> ART IN MOTION
• Invisible Information • Global Positioning
System (GPS)

> VIRTUAL LAB
• Wave or Particle? Exploring the Properties
of Light

Enter the Lab zone for hands-on inquiry.

Chapter Lab Investigation:
• Directed Inquiry: Changing Colors
• Open Inquiry: Changing Colors

Inquiry Warm-Ups: • How Do Colors Mix?
• How Does Your Reflection Wink? • How
Can You Make an Image Appear? • Can You
See Everything With One Eye? • How Does a
Pinhole Camera Work?

Quick Labs: • Developing Hypotheses
• Observing • Mirror Images • Bent Pencil
• Looking at Images • True Colors • What
a View!

my science online.com

Go to MyScienceOnline.com to
interact with this chapter's content.
Keyword: **Light**

> UNTAMED SCIENCE
• Why Is the Ocean Blue?

> PLANET DIARY
• Light

> INTERACTIVE ART
• Mirrors and Lenses • Refracting and
Reflecting Telescopes

> ART IN MOTION
• Refraction, Reflection, and Rainbows

> VIRTUAL LAB
• Color in Light

interactive SCIENCE

This is your book.
You can write in it!

THE BIG ?

Get Engaged!
At the start of each chapter, you will see two questions: an Engaging Question and the Big Question. Each chapter's Big Question will help you start thinking about the Big Ideas of Science. Look for the Big Q symbol throughout the chapter!

HOW CAN WIND KEEP YOUR LIGHTS ON?

THE BIG ?

What are some of Earth's energy sources?

This man is repairing a wind turbine at a wind farm in Texas. Most wind turbines are at least 30 meters off the ground where the winds are fast. Wind speed and blade length help determine the best way to capture the wind and turn it into power. ⊘ Develop Hypotheses Why do you think people are working to increase the amount of power we get from wind?

Wind energy collected by the turbine does not cause air pollution.

174 Energy Resources

> UNTAMED SCIENCE Watch the **Untamed Science** video to learn more about energy resources.

Untamed Science™

Follow the Untamed Science video crew as they travel the globe exploring the Big Ideas of Science.

Interact with your textbook.   Interact with inquiry.   Interact online.

Energy Resources **CHAPTER 5**

Build Reading, Inquiry, and Vocabulary Skills

In every lesson you will learn new ↻ Reading and ▲ Inquiry skills. These will help you read and think like a scientist. Vocabulary skills will help you communicate more effectively and uncover the meaning of words.

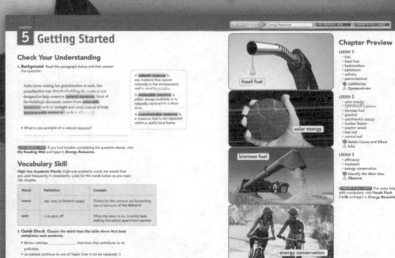

> Energy Resources   > UNTAMED SCIENCE   > THE BIG QUESTION

MY SCIENCE online.com

Go Online!

Look for the MyScienceOnline.com technology options. At MyScienceOnline.com you can immerse yourself in amazing virtual environments, get extra practice, and even blog about current events in science.

Explore the Key Concepts.

Each lesson begins with a series of Key Concept questions. The interactivities in each lesson will help you understand these concepts and Unlock the Big Question.

MY PLANET DIARY

At the start of each lesson, My Planet Diary will introduce you to amazing events, significant people, and important discoveries in science or help you to overcome common misconceptions about science concepts.

Desertification If the soil in a ___ of moisture and nutrients, the are___ advance of desertlike conditions ___ fertile is called **desertification** (d___

One cause of desertification is ___ is a period when less rain than no___ droughts, crops fail. Without pla___ blows away. Overgrazing of grass___ cutting down trees for firewood ___

Desertification is a serious pro___ and graze livestock where deserti___ people may face famine and starv___ central Africa. Millions of rural p___ cities because they can no longer ___

apply it!

Desertification affects many areas around the world.

❶ **Name** Which continent has the most existing desert?

❷ **Interpret Maps** Where in the United States is the greatest risk of desertification?

❸ **Infer** Is desertification a threa___ is existing desert? Explain. Circle ___ your answer.

❹ **CHALLENGE** If an area is facing ___ things people could do to possibl___

132 Land, Air, and Water Resour___

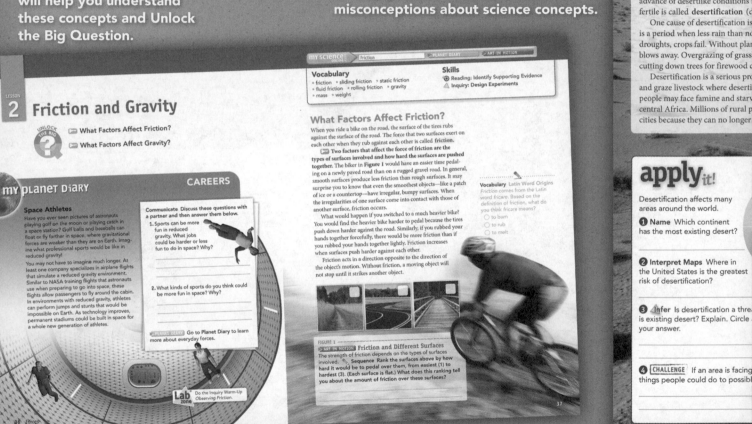

Explain what you know.

Look for the pencil. When you see it, it's time to interact with your book and demonstrate what you have learned.

apply it!

Elaborate further with the Apply It activities. This is your opportunity to take what you've learned and apply those skills to new situations.

Lab Zone

Look for the Lab zone triangle. This means it's time to do a hands-on inquiry lab. In every lesson, you'll have the opportunity to do a hands-on inquiry activity that will help reinforce your understanding of the lesson topic.

...rtile area becomes depleted ...ecome a desert. The ...as that previously were ...uh fih KAY shun). ...e. For example, a **drought** ...lls in an area. During ..., the exposed soil easily ...y cattle and sheep and ...e desertification, too. ...People cannot grow crops ...has occurred. As a result, ...Desertification is severe in ...here are moving to the ...t themselves on the land.

Key
■ Existing desert
■ High-risk area
■ Moderate-risk area

...n areas where there ...on the map to support

...fication, what are some ...ts effects?

Land Reclamation Fortunately, it is possible to replace land damaged by erosion or mining. The process of restoring an area of land to a more productive state is called **land reclamation**. In addition to restoring land for agriculture, land reclamation can restore habitats for wildlife. Many different types of land reclamation projects are currently underway all over the world. But it is generally more difficult and expensive to restore damaged land and soil than it is to protect those resources in the first place. In some cases, the land may not return to its original state.

FIGURE 4 ·············
Land Reclamation
These pictures show land before and after it was mined.

✎ **Communicate** Below the pictures, write a story about what happened to the land.

Lab zone   Do the Quick Lab Modeling ...

📖 **Assess Your Understanding**

1a. Review Subsoil has (less/more) plant and animal matter than topsoil.

b. Explain What can happen to soil if plants are removed?

c. Apply Concepts ...
that could prov... land reclam...

got it? ·······························

○ I get it! Now I know that soil management is important becau...

○ I need extra help with _____

Go to MY SCIENCE 🌐 COACH online for help with this subject.

got it?

Evaluate Your Progress.

After answering the Got It question, think about how you're doing. Did you get it or do you need a little help? Remember, MY SCIENCE ⑤ COACH is there for you if you need extra help.

Explore the Big Question.

At one point in the chapter, you'll have the opportunity to take all that you've learned to further explore the Big Question.

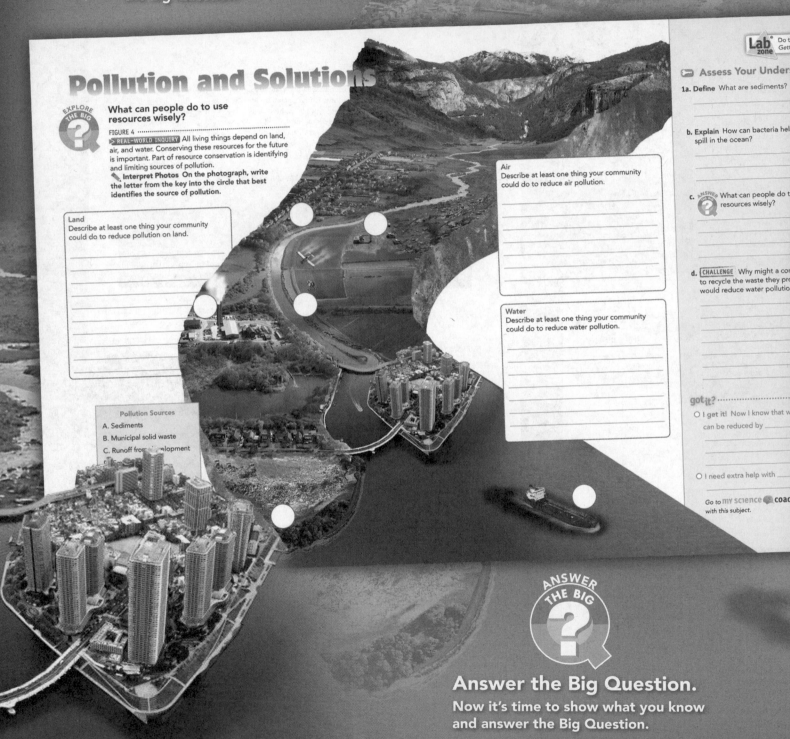

Pollution and Solutions

EXPLORE THE BIG

What can people do to use resources wisely?

FIGURE 4 ············

▶ **REAL-WORLD INQUIRY** All living things depend on land, air, and water. Conserving these resources for the future is important. Part of resource conservation is identifying and limiting sources of pollution.

✎ **Interpret Photos** On the photograph, write the letter from the key into the circle that best identifies the source of pollution.

Land
Describe at least one thing your community could do to reduce pollution on land.

Air
Describe at least one thing your community could do to reduce air pollution.

Water
Describe at least one thing your community could do to reduce water pollution.

Pollution Sources
A. Sediments
B. Municipal solid waste
C. Runoff from development

Lab zone Do th
Getti

🔒 **Assess Your Unders**

1a. Define What are sediments?

b. Explain How can bacteria help spill in the ocean?

c. ANSWER What can people do to resources wisely?

d. CHALLENGE Why might a con
to recycle the waste they pro
would reduce water pollutio

got it? ·············
○ I get it! Now I know that w
can be reduced by

○ I need extra help with

Go to MY SCIENCE coac
with this subject.

ANSWER THE BIG

Answer the Big Question.

Now it's time to show what you know and answer the Big Question.

Review What You've Learned.

Use the Chapter Study Guide to review the Big Question and prepare for the test.

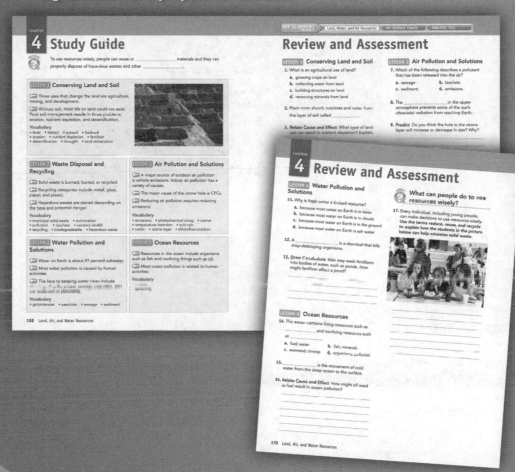

Practice Taking Tests.

Apply the Big Question and take a practice test in standardized test format.

INTERACT... WITH YOUR TEXTBOOK...

Go to MyScienceOnline.com and immerse yourself in amazing virtual environments.

THE BIG QUESTION

Each online chapter starts with a Big Question. Your mission is to unlock the meaning of this Big Question as each science lesson unfolds.

Unit 4 > Chapter 1 > Lesson 1

The Big Question | Unlock the Big Question | Explore the Big Question

The Big Question   Check Your Understanding   Vocabulary Skill

Populations and Communities

Tools

The Big Question

Unit 2 > Chapter 4 > Lesson 1

Engage & Explore | Explain

Planet Diary

my planet diary

VOCAB FLASH CARDS

Practice chapter vocabulary with interactive flash cards. Each card has an image, definitions in English and Spanish, and space for your own notes.

Unit 4 > Chapter 1 > Lesson 1

The Big Question | Unlock the Big Question | Explore the Big Question

The Big Question   Untamed Science   Check Your Understanding   Vocabulary Skill   Vocabulary Flashcards

Vocabulary Flashcards

Tools

Card List | Create-a-Card   10 Cards Left | Test Me

Lesson Cards | My Cards

Birth Rate
Carrying Capacity
Commensalism
Community
Competition
Death Rate
Ecology
Ecosystem
Emigration
Habitat
Host
Immigration
Limiting Factor

Science Vocabulary

Term: **Community**

Definition: **All the different populations that live together in a particular area.**

View Spanish

Add Notes

Card 5 of

Unit 6 > Chapter 1 > Lesson 3

Engage & Explore | Ex

Apply It   Directed Virtual Lab

Color in Light

Exit

Reset Lab

Unit 6 > Chapter 1 > Lesson 1

Engage & Explore | Explain | Elaborate | Evaluate

Apply It   Do the Math   Art in Motion   Interactive Art   Real World Inquiry

The Nebraska Plains

▶ Bald Eagle

Information | Media

Haliaeetus leucocephalus
Bald Eagles are 80-95 cm tall with a wingspan of 180-230 cm. These birds are born with all brown feathers but grow white feathers on their head, neck, and tail.

Layers List   ▲ Show

Next

22 of 22

Back

INTERACTIVE ART

At MyScienceOnline.com, many of the beautiful visuals in your book become interactive so you can extend your learning.

WITH INQUIRY...

GO ONLINE

my science online.com > Populations and Communities > **PLANET DIARY** > **LAB ZONE** > **VIRTUAL LAB**

> PLANET DIARY

My Planet Diary online is the place to find more information and activities related to the topic in the lesson.

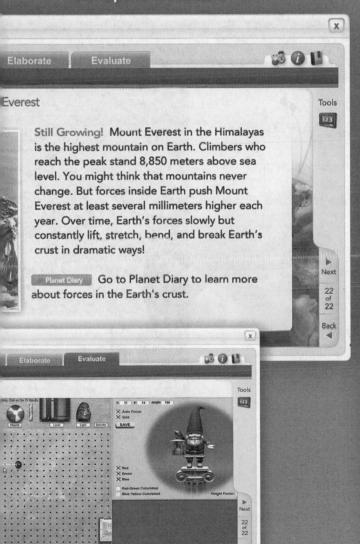

Elaborate | Evaluate

Everest

Tools

Still Growing! Mount Everest in the Himalayas is the highest mountain on Earth. Climbers who reach the peak stand 8,850 meters above sea level. You might think that mountains never change. But forces inside Earth push Mount Everest at least several millimeters higher each year. Over time, Earth's forces slowly but constantly lift, stretch, bend, and break Earth's crust in dramatic ways!

Planet Diary Go to Planet Diary to learn more about forces in the Earth's crust.

Next

22 of 22

Back

Elaborate | Evaluate

Tools

Next

22 of 22

Back

0:35 / 1:30

> VIRTUAL LAB

Get more practice with realistic virtual labs. Manipulate the variables on-screen and test your hypothesis.

⟳ + http://www.myscienceonline.com/

Find Your Chapter

1 Go to www.myscienceonline.com.

2 Log in with username and password.

3 Click on your program and select your chapter.

Keyword Search

1 Go to www.myscienceonline.com.

2 Log in with username and password.

3 Click on your program and select Search.

4 Enter the keyword (from your book) in the search box.

Other Content Available Online

> UNTAMED SCIENCE Follow these young scientists through their amazing online video blogs as they travel the globe in search of answers to the Big Questions of Science.

> MY SCIENCE COACH Need extra help? My Science Coach is your personal online study partner. My Science Coach is a chance for you to get more practice on key science concepts. There you can choose from a variety of tools that will help guide you through each science lesson.

> MY READING WEB Need extra reading help on a particular science topic? At My Reading Web you will find a choice of reading selections targeted to your specific reading level.

? BIG IDEAS OF SCIENCE

Have you ever worked on a jigsaw puzzle? Usually a puzzle has a theme that leads you to group the pieces by what they have in common. But until you put all the pieces together you can't solve the puzzle. Studying science is similar to solving a puzzle. The big ideas of science are like puzzle themes. To understand big ideas, scientists ask questions. The answers to those questions are like pieces of a puzzle. Each chapter in this book asks a big question to help you think about a big idea of science. By answering the big questions, you will get closer to understanding the big idea.

✎ **Before you read each chapter, write about what you know and what more you'd like to know.**

Grant Wiggins, coauthor of *Understanding by Design*

The light and heat that lightning gives off travels in the form of electromagnetic waves. An electromagnetic wave consists of vibrating electric and magnetic fields that move through space at the speed of light—about 300,000 kilometers per second.

BIGIDEA

Waves transmit energy.

What do you already know about waves and how they travel from one place to another?
✎ **What more would you like to know?**

_____

_____

_____

_____

Big Question:

❓ What are the properties of waves? Chapter 1

❓ What determines the pitch and loudness of sound? Chapter 2

❓ What kinds of waves make up the electromagnetic spectrum? Chapter 3

❓ How does light interact with matter? Chapter 4

✎ **After reading the chapters, write what you have learned about the Big Idea.**

_____

_____

_____

_____

Electric field

Direction
of wave

Magnetic field

90°

Fields are at
right angles
to each other.

HOW WOULD YOU DESCRIBE WAVES?

THE BIG ?

What are the properties of waves?

Imagine a sunny day on a calm sea. It seems as if you can see to the edge of the world. Suddenly, the clouds roll in, and the waves begin to get larger and faster. Soon, you can barely see past the next wave. One after another, they batter the sailboat, making it pitch and roll like a wild roller coaster. **Draw Conclusions** What are some features of waves?

_____

_____

_____

_____

_____

_____

▶ **UNTAMED SCIENCE** Watch the **Untamed Science** video to learn more about waves.

Characteristics of Waves

1 Getting Started

Check Your Understanding

1. **Background** Read the paragraph below and then answer the question.

At a public pond, Lionel skips stones and tosses rocks into the water, sending waves in all directions. Nearby, Ali **floats** a wooden boat. Both boys observe the **properties** of the waves. The rocks make higher waves than the stones. They watch the **interaction** of the waves and the boat. The boat bounces violently as the higher waves travel under it.

Something **floats** if it moves or rests on the surface of a liquid without sinking.

The **properties** of something are its characteristic qualities or features.

Interaction is the combined action or effect that things have on each other.

- What example in the paragraph suggests that the properties of waves might affect a floating object?

_____

_____

_____

> MY READING WEB If you had trouble completing the question above, visit **My Reading Web** and type in *Characteristics of Waves*.

Vocabulary Skill

Identify Multiple Meanings Some words have more than one meaning. Consider the everyday and scientific meanings of the words below.

Word	Everyday Meaning	Scientific Meaning
reflection	*n.* serious thought or consideration	*n.* the bouncing back of a wave from a surface
frequency	*n.* the rate at which something occurs	*n.* the number of waves that pass a point in a certain time

2. **Quick Check** Circle in the chart the meaning of *reflection* as it is used in the following sentence: An echo is the *reflection* of a sound wave.

wave

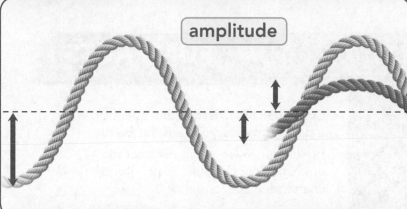

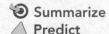

amplitude

reflection

refraction

Chapter Preview

LESSON 1
- wave
- energy
- medium
- mechanical wave
- vibration
- transverse wave
- crest
- trough
- longitudinal wave
- compression
- rarefaction

🔄 **Summarize**
△ **Predict**

LESSON 2
- amplitude
- wavelength
- frequency
- hertz

🔄 **Identify the Main Idea**
△ **Calculate**

LESSON 3
- reflection
- refraction
- diffraction
- interference
- constructive interference
- destructive interference
- standing wave
- node
- antinode
- resonance

🔄 **Relate Cause and Effect**
△ **Observe**

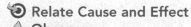 ▷ **VOCAB FLASH CARDS** For extra help with vocabulary, visit **Vocab Flash Cards** and type in *Characteristics of Waves.*

3

What Are Waves?

UNLOCK THE BIG ?

🔑 **What Forms Mechanical Waves?**

🔑 **What Are the Types of Mechanical Waves?**

my planet Diary

The Power of Waves

Where does the energy that powers your school come from? It may be from oil, gas, or coal. You also may have heard of using the sun or wind as energy sources. But did you know that ocean waves could be used as an energy source, too? Mechanical systems placed in the ocean or along the shore transform the energy from waves into electricity. Unlike oil, gas, or coal, the energy from ocean waves will not run out. Although wave energy technology is still very new, many scientists are optimistic about its possible use around the world.

FUN FACTS

Communicate Discuss this question with a partner. Write your answer below.

How might wave energy impact the environment? Consider both intended and unintended consequences.

_____

_____

_____

_____

_____

_____

▶ PLANET DIARY Go to **Planet Diary** to learn more about waves.

Lab zone® Do the Inquiry Warm-Up *What Are Waves?*

Vocabulary

- wave • energy • medium • mechanical wave
- vibration • transverse wave • crest • trough
- longitudinal wave • compression • rarefaction

Skills

↻ Reading: Summarize

△ Inquiry: Predict

What Forms Mechanical Waves?

You have probably seen and felt water waves while swimming. But did you know that many kinds of waves affect you daily? Sound and light are very different from water waves, but they are waves, too.

Characteristics of Waves What is a wave? A **wave** is a disturbance involving the transfer of energy from place to place. In science, **energy** is defined as the ability to do work. For example, the energy of a water wave can lift an object on the water's surface as the wave passes under it. But after the wave passes, the water is calm again.

Most waves need something to travel through. For example, sound waves can travel through air, water, and even solid materials. Water waves travel along the surface of the water. A wave can even travel along an object, such as a rope. The material through which a wave travels is called a **medium.** Gases (such as air), liquids (such as water), and solids (such as ropes) can all act as mediums. Waves that require a medium to travel are called **mechanical waves**.

✎ **Summarize** On the notebook paper, summarize the text on this page in your own words.

CHALLENGE The news media, such as newspapers and television stations, carry current events worldwide. Explain how the way news travels is similar to the way a wave travels.

_____

_____

_____

_____

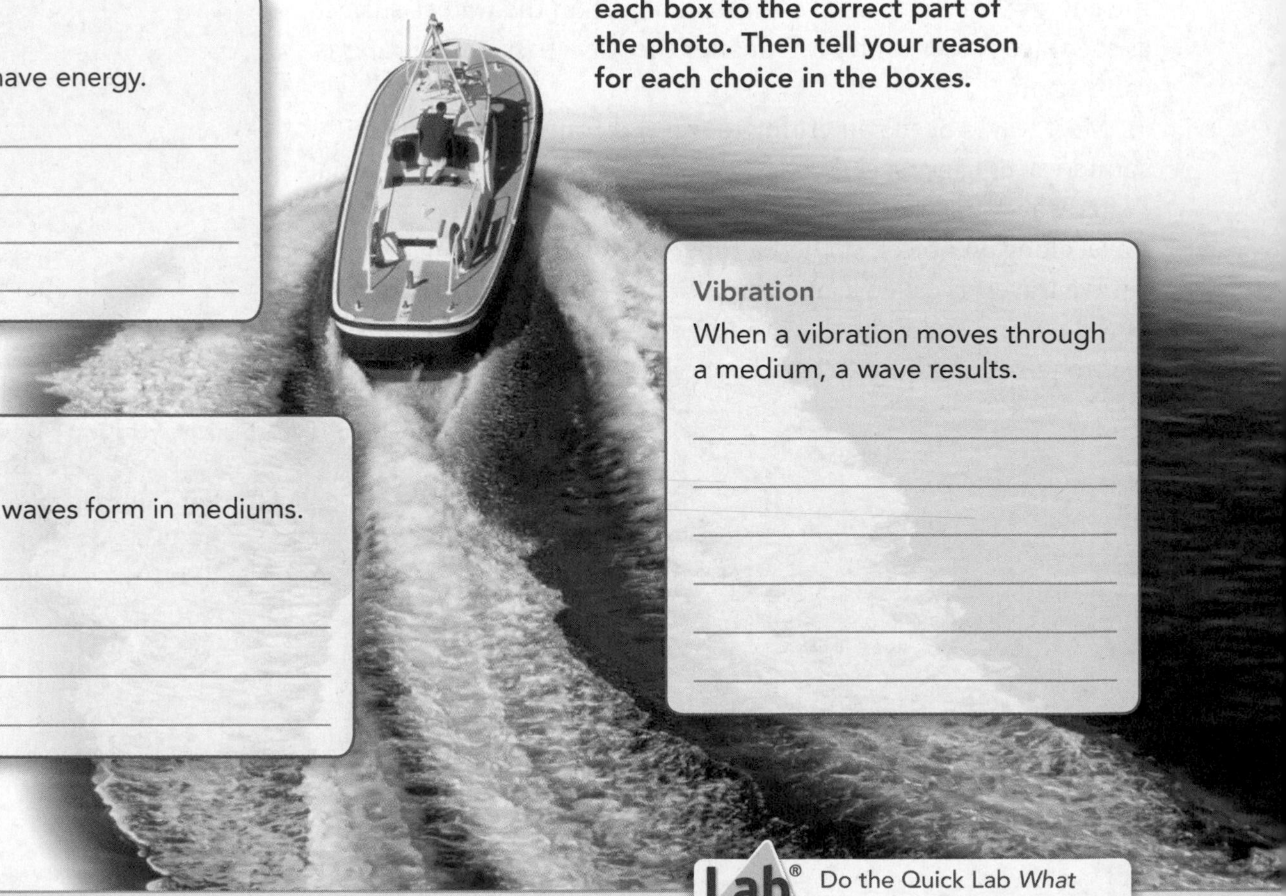

Energy Source

Moving objects have energy.

_____

_____

_____

Medium

Mechanical waves form in mediums.

_____

_____

_____

_____

Waves and Energy

Energy is needed to make a wave. **Mechanical waves form when a source of energy causes a medium to vibrate.** A **vibration** is a repeated back-and-forth or up-and-down motion. Moving objects have energy, which they can transfer to a medium to produce waves. For example, as you see in **Figure 1,** a motorboat's propeller can transfer energy to calm water. As a result, the particles that make up the water start to vibrate. The vibrations move through the water, resulting in a wave.

FIGURE 1 ···

Forming a Mechanical Wave

A source of energy in a medium can cause a mechanical wave to form.

Explain Draw an arrow from each box to the correct part of the photo. Then tell your reason for each choice in the boxes.

Vibration

When a vibration moves through a medium, a wave results.

_____

_____

_____

_____

_____

Lab zone® Do the Quick Lab *What Causes Mechanical Waves?*

Assess Your Understanding

got it? ··

○ **I get it!** Now I know that a mechanical wave forms when _____

_____

○ **I need extra help with** _____

Go to **MY SCIENCE COACH** online for help with this subject.

What Are the Types of Mechanical Waves?

Waves move through mediums in different ways. **The three types of mechanical waves are transverse waves, longitudinal waves, and surface waves.** These waves are classified by how they move through mediums.

Transverse Waves When you make a wave on a rope, the wave moves from one end of the rope to the other. However, the rope itself moves up and down or from side to side, at right angles to the direction in which the wave travels. A wave that vibrates the medium at right angles, or perpendicular, to the direction in which the wave travels is called a **transverse wave.**

Making a transverse wave on a rope forms high and low points along the rope. A high point on a transverse wave is called a **crest,** and a low point is called a **trough** (trawf). In **Figure 2,** you can see that the red ribbon on the rope is first at a crest and then at a trough. As the wave moves through the rope, the ribbon moves up and down between crests and troughs. The dashed line shows the rope's position before it was moved. It is called the rest position.

Vocabulary Identify Multiple Meanings The word *trough* has more than one meaning. Write two sentences that use the word, one showing its everyday meaning and one showing its scientific meaning.

_____

_____

_____

_____

FIGURE 2 ·····················

Motion in a Transverse Wave

When you shake out a bedsheet or move a rope up and down, you create a transverse wave.

✎ Complete the tasks.

1. **Identify** Label the crest, trough, and rest position.
2. **Relate Text and Visuals** Draw a vertical line through the purple arrows and a horizontal line through the blue arrow until it touches the vertical line. What angle did you draw?

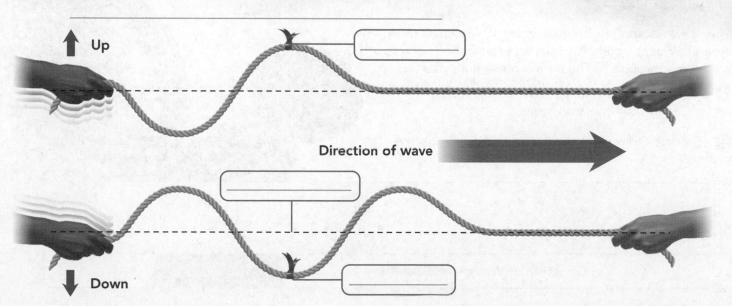

Up

Direction of wave

Down

7

FIGURE 3

Motion in a Longitudinal Wave

Fixed points on a transverse wave vibrate up and down. Fixed points on a longitudinal wave, such as the one marked by the red ribbon, vibrate back and forth.

✏ **Interpret Diagrams** Label the areas of compression and rarefaction in the diagram.

Longitudinal Waves If you push and pull one end of a spring toy, you can produce a longitudinal wave like the one shown in **Figure 3**. Notice that the coils in the spring move back and forth in the same direction, or parallel, to the wave's motion. A **longitudinal wave** (lawn juh TOO duh nul) vibrates the medium in the same direction in which the wave travels. Also, notice how the spacing between the coils varies. Some coils are close together, while others are farther apart. An area where the coils are close together is called a **compression** (kum PRESH un). An area where the coils are spread out is called a **rarefaction** (rair uh FAK shun).

As compressions and rarefactions travel along the spring toy, each coil moves forward and then back. The energy travels from one end of the spring to the other, in the form of a wave. After the wave passes, each coil returns to its starting position.

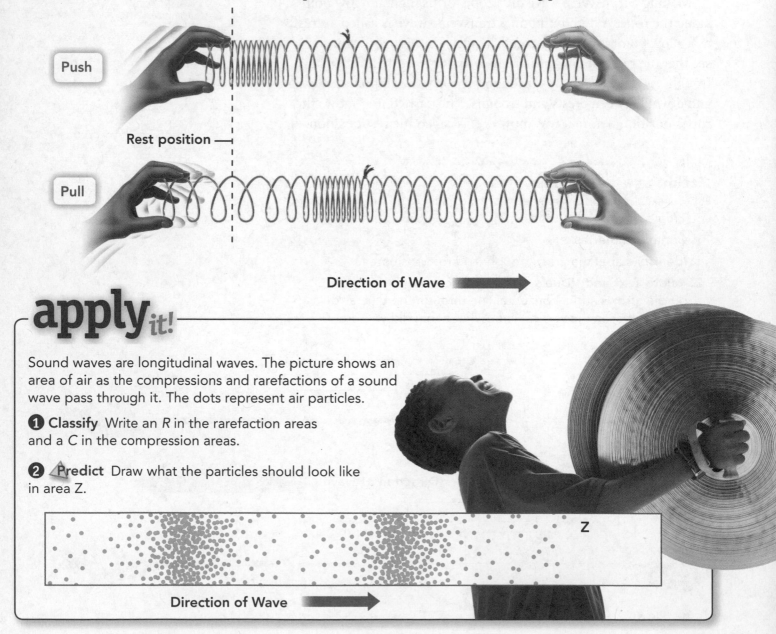

Push

Rest position —

Pull

Direction of Wave ➡

apply it!

Sound waves are longitudinal waves. The picture shows an area of air as the compressions and rarefactions of a sound wave pass through it. The dots represent air particles.

❶ **Classify** Write an *R* in the rarefaction areas and a *C* in the compression areas.

❷ **Predict** Draw what the particles should look like in area Z.

Z

Direction of Wave ➡

Surface Waves

Surface Waves Surface waves are combinations of transverse and longitudinal waves. This type of wave travels along a surface that separates two mediums. Ocean waves are the most familiar surface wave. An ocean wave travels at the surface between water and air. When a wave passes through water, the water (and anything on it) vibrates up and down, like a transverse wave on a rope. The water also moves back and forth slightly in the direction that the wave is traveling, like the coils of a spring. But unlike the coils of a spring, water does not compress. The up-and-down and back-and-forth movements combine to make each particle of water move in a circle, as you see in **Figure 4.**

FIGURE 4 ·······························

▶ **ART IN MOTION** **Waves Transfer Energy**
A wave moves the bottle in a circular motion. After the wave passes, the bottle returns to where it started.

✏️ **Predict** In the empty box, draw what the next picture should look like.

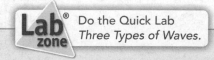
Do the Quick Lab
Three Types of Waves.

🔑 Assess Your Understanding

1a. Review Compared to the direction it travels, at what angle does a transverse wave vibrate a medium?

_____

_____

b. Compare and Contrast How are transverse and longitudinal waves alike and different?

_____

_____

got it?

○ I get it! Now I know that the three types of mechanical waves are _____

_____

_____

_____

○ I need extra help with _____

Go to MY SCIENCE ⓢ COACH *online for help with this subject.*

9

Properties of Waves

UNLOCK THE BIG

🔑 **What Are the Amplitude, Wavelength, Frequency, and Speed of a Wave?**

🔑 **How Are Frequency, Wavelength, and Speed Related?**

MY PLANET DIARY

DISCOVERY

The Sound of Romance

Bzzzzzzzzz! Bzzzzzzzzz! What's that noise? It's the sound of a mosquito buzzing in your ear. This distinct buzzing sound comes from sound waves formed as a mosquito beats its wings. Researchers recently discovered that the buzzing sound of female mosquitoes attracts male mosquitoes. When a male mosquito meets a female, he quickly adjusts his own buzz to match the frequency of the sound waves created by the female. Researchers think that this matched buzzing frequency aids in mosquito mating.

Communicate Discuss this question with a partner. Write your answer below.

What are two other animals you know of that make buzzing sounds?

_____

_____

_____

_____

_____

_____

_____

▶ PLANET DIARY Go to **Planet Diary** to learn more about wave properties.

Lab zone® Do the Inquiry Warm-Up *What Do Waves Look Like?*

Vocabulary
- amplitude • wavelength • frequency • hertz

Skills
↻ Reading: Identify the Main Idea
△ Inquiry: Calculate

What Are the Amplitude, Wavelength, Frequency, and Speed of a Wave?

Waves may vary greatly. For example, waves can be long or short. They can carry a little energy or a lot of energy. They can be transverse or longitudinal. However, all waves have common properties—amplitude, wavelength, frequency, and speed. 🔑 **Amplitude describes how far the medium in a wave moves. Wavelength describes a wave's length, and frequency describes how often it occurs. Speed describes how quickly a wave moves.**

Amplitude The height of a wave's crest depends on its amplitude. **Amplitude** is the maximum distance the medium vibrates from the rest position. For a water wave, this distance is how far the water particles move above or below the surface level of calm water. High waves have more energy than low waves. The more energy a wave has, the greater its amplitude.

A transverse wave is shown in **Figure 1.** Its amplitude is the maximum distance the medium moves up or down from its rest position. The amplitude of a longitudinal wave is a measure of how compressed or rarefied the medium becomes. When the compressions are dense, it means the wave's amplitude is large.

FIGURE 1 ··
Amplitude
The amplitude of a transverse wave is the maximum distance the medium vibrates from the rest position.

✏ **Label the parts of the wave. Then answer the question.**
Measure What is the amplitude of the wave in centimeters?

_____

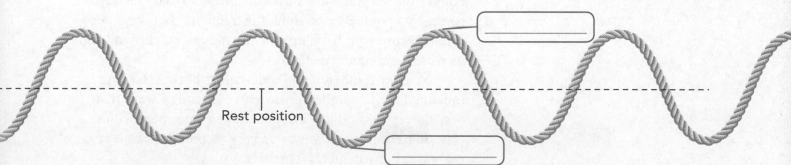

Rest position

FIGURE 2 ···

Properties of Waves

All waves have amplitude, wavelength, frequency, and speed.

✎ **Read the text on these pages before filling in the boxes and answering these questions.**

1. **Name** Which transverse wave has the shortest wavelength?

_____

_____

2. **Apply Concepts** If a transverse wave travels 10 meters in 5 seconds, what is its speed?

_____

3. **Draw Conclusions** How does a shorter wavelength affect the frequency of a wave?

_____

_____

_____

_____

_____

_____

_____

_____

✎ **Identify the Main Idea** Read the text. Underline the main idea in each of the three sections.

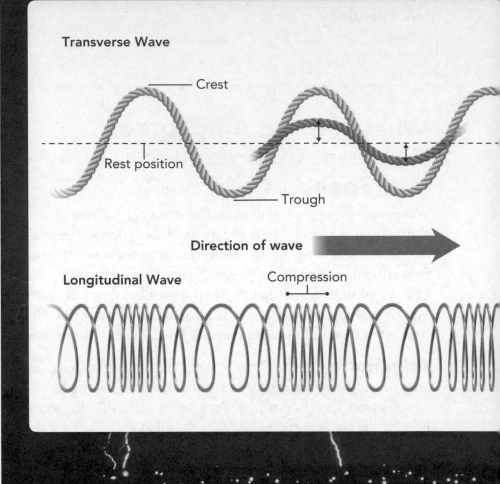

Transverse Wave

Crest

Rest position

Trough

Direction of wave

Longitudinal Wave

Compression

Wavelength A wave travels a certain distance before it starts to repeat. The distance between two corresponding parts of a wave is its **wavelength.** You can find the wavelength of a transverse wave by measuring the distance from crest to crest as shown in **Figure 2.** For a longitudinal wave, the wavelength is the distance between compressions.

Frequency The **frequency** of a wave is the number of waves that pass a given point in a certain amount of time. For example, if you make waves on a rope so that one wave passes by a point every second, the frequency is 1 wave per second. Move your hand up and down more quickly and you increase the frequency.

Frequency is measured in units called **hertz** (Hz), and is defined as the number of waves per second. A wave that occurs every second has a frequency of 1 wave per second (1/s) or 1 Hz. If two waves pass every second the frequency is 2 waves per second (2/s) or 2 Hz.

Which wave has the greater amplitude—yellow or blue?

_____

_____

One yellow wave passes this point each second, so the frequency is _____.

Wavelength

Amplitude

Wavelength

Two green waves pass this point each second, so the frequency is _____.

Wavelength

Rarefaction

Speed Different waves travel at different speeds. Think about watching a distant thunderstorm on a hot summer day. The thunder occurs the instant the lightning flashes, but the light and sound reach you seconds apart. This happens because light waves travel much faster than sound waves. In fact, light waves travel about a million times faster than sound waves!

The speed of a wave is how far the wave travels in a given amount of time. You can determine a wave's speed by dividing the distance it travels by the time it takes to travel that distance. Sound, for example, travels about 990 meters in 3 seconds in air when the temperature is 0°C. Therefore, its speed is 330 m/s in these conditions. As long as the temperature of the medium (air) doesn't change, the speed of sound will stay the same.

Do the Quick Lab
Properties of Waves.

Assess Your Understanding

got it? ....

○ **I get it!** Now I know that for any wave,

amplitude describes _____

_____,

wavelength describes _____,

frequency describes _____

_____,

and speed describes _____

_____

○ **I need extra help with** _____

Go to MY SCIENCE COACH *online for help with this subject.*

How Are Frequency, Wavelength, and Speed Related?

You just learned that you can calculate the speed of a wave by dividing the distance it travels by the time it takes to travel that distance. But you can also calculate the speed of a wave if you know its wavelength and frequency. 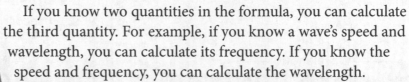 **The speed, wavelength, and frequency of a wave are related by a mathematical formula.**

$$\text{Speed} = \text{Wavelength} \times \text{Frequency}$$

If you know two quantities in the formula, you can calculate the third quantity. For example, if you know a wave's speed and wavelength, you can calculate its frequency. If you know the speed and frequency, you can calculate the wavelength.

$$\text{Frequency} = \frac{\text{Speed}}{\text{Wavelength}}$$

$$\text{Wavelength} = \frac{\text{Speed}}{\text{Frequency}}$$

The speed of a wave remains constant if the medium, temperature, and pressure do not change. For example, all sound waves travel at the same speed in air at a given temperature and pressure. Even if a sound wave's frequency changes, its speed stays the same. So, if the frequency of a sound wave increases, its wavelength must decrease to maintain a constant speed.

do the math!

The table shows measurements of some properties of a sound wave in water and in air.

1 ◢ **Calculate** Using what you know about the relationship between wavelength, frequency, and speed, fill in the table.

2 [CHALLENGE] What can this table tell you about the speed of a wave?

Medium	Wavelength	Frequency	Speed
Water	_____	200 Hz	1500 m/s
Water	3.75 m	400 Hz	_____
Air (20°C)	10 m	_____	343 m/s
Air (20°C)	_____	17.15 Hz	343 m/s

_____

_____

_____

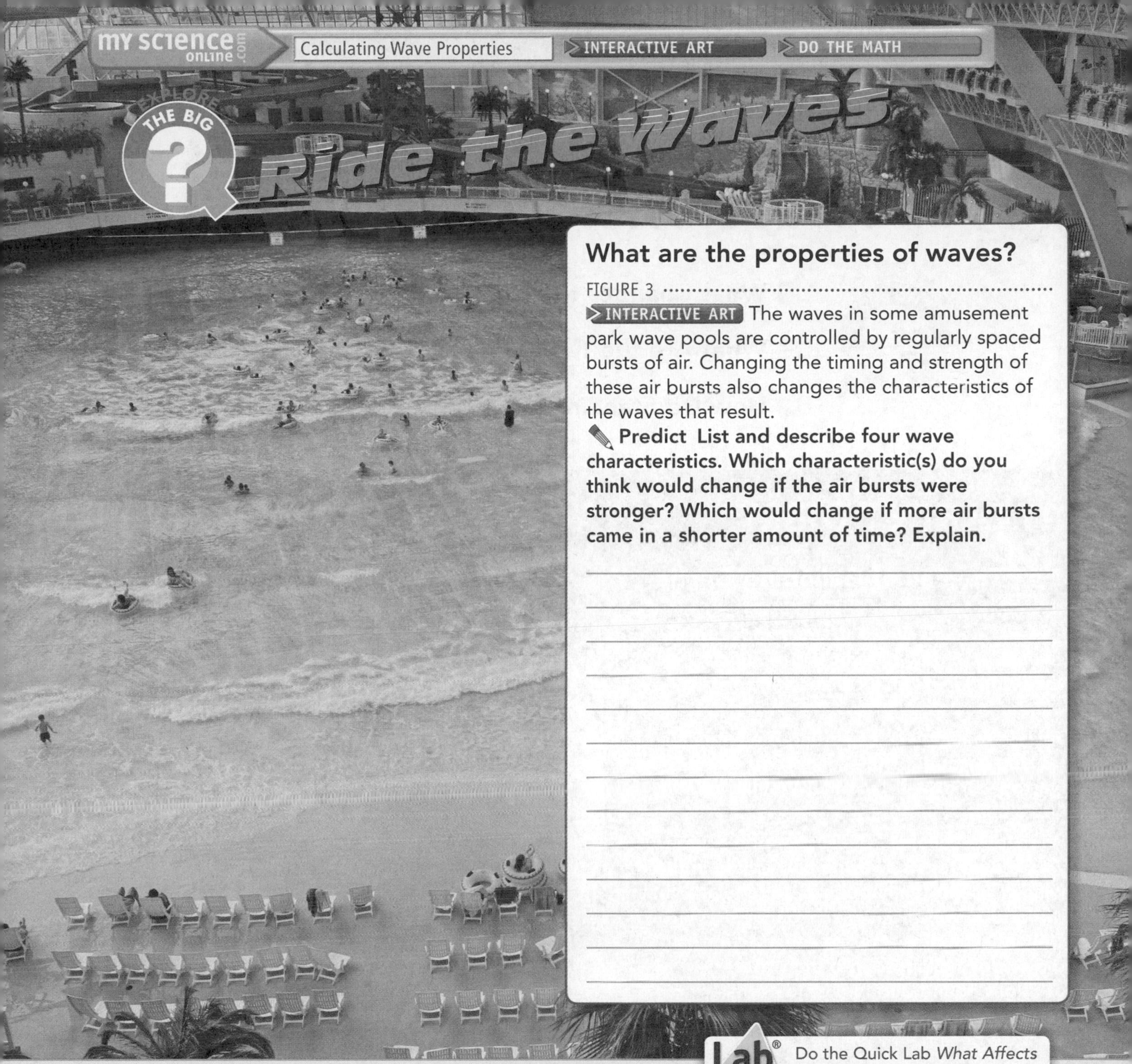

EXPLORE
THE BIG
?

Ride the Waves

What are the properties of waves?

FIGURE 3 ·······································

▷ **INTERACTIVE ART** The waves in some amusement park wave pools are controlled by regularly spaced bursts of air. Changing the timing and strength of these air bursts also changes the characteristics of the waves that result.

✎ **Predict** List and describe four wave characteristics. Which characteristic(s) do you think would change if the air bursts were stronger? Which would change if more air bursts came in a shorter amount of time? Explain.

_____

_____

_____

_____

_____

_____

_____

_____

_____

_____

_____

_____

_____

Lab zone®   Do the Quick Lab *What Affects the Speed of a Wave?*

🔑 Assess Your Understanding

1a. ANSWER THE BIG **?** What are the properties of waves?

_____

_____

b. Calculate A wave's frequency is 2 Hz and its wavelength is 4 m. What is the wave's speed?

_____

got it?

◯ I get it! Now I know that wavelength, frequency, and speed are related by the formula _____

_____

◯ I need extra help with _____

Go to **MY SCIENCE** 🔊 **COACH** *online for help with this subject.*

15

Interactions of Waves

🗝 **What Changes the Direction of a Wave?**

🗝 **What Are the Two Types of Wave Interference?**

🗝 **How Do Standing Waves Form?**

my planet diary

DISASTER

The Fall of Galloping Gertie

"My breath was coming in gasps; my knees were raw and bleeding, my hands bruised and swollen.... Safely back at the toll plaza, I saw the bridge in its final collapse and saw my car plunge into the Narrows."

This dramatic piece of writing is a witness's real-life account of the collapse of the Tacoma Narrows Bridge in Tacoma, Washington, on November 7, 1940.

Prior to its collapse, the suspension bridge was known for its swaying and rolling in the wind. This motion happened so regularly that the bridge was nicknamed "Galloping Gertie." Only four months after its construction, the bridge collapsed into the waters of Puget Sound during a windstorm. Although a disaster, Galloping Gertie's collapse became a valuable teaching tool for engineers.

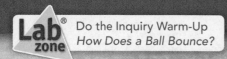

Lab zone Do the Inquiry Warm-Up *How Does a Ball Bounce?*

Communicate Discuss the following questions with a partner. Write your answers below.

1. Why is "Galloping Gertie" an appropriate nickname for the bridge?

_____

_____

2. If you were an engineer studying this bridge collapse, what is one thing you would research?

_____

_____

▷ **PLANET DIARY** Go to **Planet Diary** to learn more about waves interacting.

Vocabulary

- reflection • refraction • diffraction • interference
- constructive interference • destructive interference
- standing wave • node • antinode • resonance

Skills

⟳ Reading: Relate Cause and Effect

△ Inquiry: Observe

What Changes the Direction of a Wave?

If you toss a ball against a wall, the ball bounces back in a new direction. Like a ball, waves can also change direction. 🔑 **Waves change direction by reflection, refraction, and diffraction.**

Reflection When a wave hits a surface, any part of the wave that cannot pass through the surface bounces back. This interaction with a surface is called **reflection.** Reflection happens often in your everyday life. When you looked in your mirror this morning you used reflected light to see yourself. The echo you hear when you shout in an empty gym is also a reflection.

In **Figure 1** you can see how light waves are reflected. All reflected waves obey the law of reflection.

FIGURE 1 ·······················

The Law of Reflection
The law of reflection states that the angle of incidence equals the angle of reflection.

✎ **Explain** Read the sequence of steps, matching each step to its letter in the photo. If the angle of incidence is 45°, explain what the angle of reflection would be.

_____

_____

_____

_____

_____

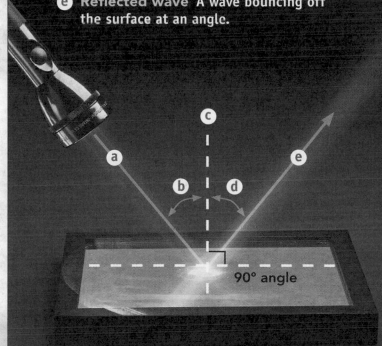

ⓐ **Incoming wave** A wave moving toward the surface at an angle.

ⓑ **Angle of incidence** The angle between the incoming wave and the normal.

ⓒ **Normal** A line perpendicular to the surface at the point where reflection occurs.

ⓓ **Angle of reflection** The angle between the reflected wave and the normal.

ⓔ **Reflected wave** A wave bouncing off the surface at an angle.

90° angle

Refraction

Have you ever ridden a skateboard and gone off the sidewalk onto grass? If so, you know it's hard to keep moving in a straight line. The front wheel on the side moving onto the grass slows down. The front wheel still on the sidewalk continues to move fast. The difference in the speeds of the two front wheels causes the skateboard to change direction.

Like a skateboard that changes direction, changes in speed can cause waves to change direction. Look at **Figure 2.** When a wave enters a new medium at an angle, one side of the wave changes speed before the other side. This causes the wave to bend. Bending occurs because different parts of the wave travel at different speeds. **Refraction** is the bending of waves due to a change in speed.

Waves do not always bend when entering a new medium. No bending occurs if a wave enters a new medium at a right angle. Bending does not occur if the speed of the wave in the new medium is the same as the speed of the wave in the old medium.

↪ **Relate Cause and Effect**
In the second paragraph, circle the cause of refraction and underline the effect of refraction.

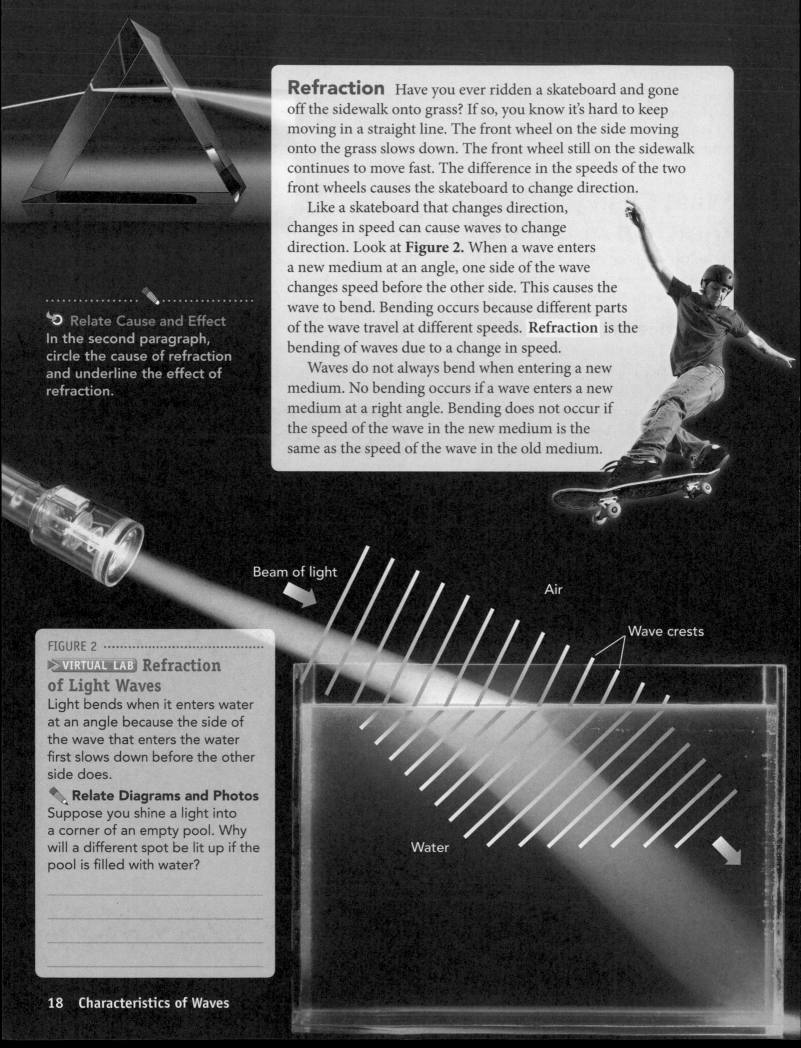

Beam of light

Air

Wave crests

Water

FIGURE 2 ······
▶ VIRTUAL LAB **Refraction of Light Waves**
Light bends when it enters water at an angle because the side of the wave that enters the water first slows down before the other side does.

✎ **Relate Diagrams and Photos**
Suppose you shine a light into a corner of an empty pool. Why will a different spot be lit up if the pool is filled with water?

_____

_____

_____

_____

Diffraction Waves sometimes bend around barriers or pass through openings. When a wave moves around a barrier or through an opening in a barrier, it bends and spreads out. These wave interactions are called **diffraction.** Two examples of diffraction are shown in **Figure 3.**

FIGURE 3 ⋯⋯⋯⋯⋯⋯⋯
The Diffraction of Water Waves
Water waves diffract when they encounter canals or shorelines.

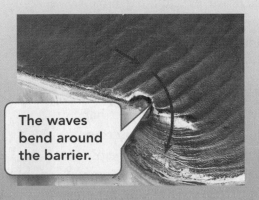

The waves bend around the barrier.

The waves spread out after passing through the narrow opening.

apply it!

Use the three pictures on the right to answer the questions.

1 **Observe** Under each picture, write how the waves are changing direction.

2 **Summarize** In what way are reflection, refraction, and diffraction similar?

_____

_____

_____

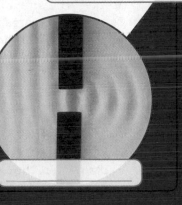

Lab zone® Do the Lab Investigation *Making Waves.*

🔑 Assess Your Understanding

1a. Define What is diffraction?

_____

_____

_____

b. Classify A wave bends after entering a new medium. What type of interaction is this?

_____

_____

got it?

○ **I get it!** Now I know that a wave's direction can be changed by _____

_____

_____

○ **I need extra help with** _____

Go to **MY SCIENCE** ⓢ **COACH** online for help with this subject.

What Are the Two Types of Wave Interference?

Have you ever seen soccer balls collide? The balls bounce off each other because they cannot be in the same place at the same time. Surprisingly, this is not true of waves. Unlike two balls, two waves can overlap when they meet. **Interference** is the interaction between waves that meet. 🔑 **There are two types of interference: constructive and destructive.**

Constructive Interference Interference in which waves combine to form a wave with a larger amplitude than any individual wave's amplitude is called **constructive interference.** You can think of constructive interference as waves "helping each other," or adding their energies. For example, in **Figure 4,** when the crests of two waves overlap, they make a higher crest. If two troughs overlap, they make a deeper trough. In both cases, the amplitude of the combined crests or troughs increases.

FIGURE 4 ·······················

Constructive Interference
✎ **Infer** Explain what the black dotted line represents. Then tell what happens to the direction of each wave when the waves meet.

_____

_____

_____

_____

_____

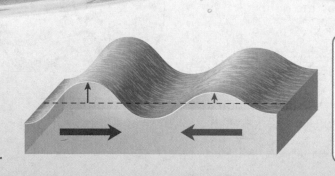

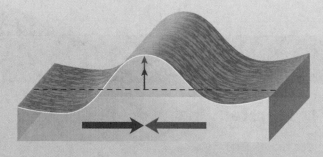

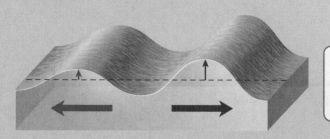

❶ Two waves approach each other. The wave on the left has a greater amplitude.

❷ The crest's new amplitude is the sum of the amplitudes of the original crests.

❸ The waves continue on as if they had not met.

Destructive Interference

Interference in which two waves combine to form a wave with a smaller amplitude than either original wave had is called **destructive interference.** Destructive interference can occur when the crest of one wave overlaps the trough of another wave. If the crest has a larger amplitude than the trough of the other wave, the crest "wins" and part of it remains. If the original trough had a larger amplitude than the crest of the other wave, the result is a trough. If a crest and trough have equal amplitudes, they will completely cancel as shown in **Figure 5.** Destructive interference is used in noise-canceling headphones to block out distracting noises in a listener's surroundings.

FIGURE 5 ·················

> INTERACTIVE ART **Destructive Interference**

✎ ✐ **Observe** Look at the pictures below. In the boxes, describe the steps of destructive interference.

1 _____

_____

_____

_____

2 _____

_____

_____

_____

3 _____

_____

_____

Lab zone® Do the Quick Lab Wave Interference.

🔑 Assess Your Understanding

got it? ·················

○ **I get it!** Now I know that the two types of wave interference are _____

_____

○ **I need extra help with** _____

Go to MY SCIENCE ○ COACH online for help with this subject.

How Do Standing Waves Form?

If you tie a rope to a doorknob and shake the free end, waves will travel down the rope, reflect at the end, and come back. The reflected waves will meet the incoming waves and interference occurs. 🔑 **If the incoming wave and reflected wave have just the right frequency, they combine to form a wave that appears to stand still. This wave is called a standing wave.** A **standing wave** is a wave that appears to stand in one place, even though it is two waves interfering as they pass through each other.

Nodes and Antinodes In a standing wave, destructive interference produces points with zero amplitude, called **nodes**, as shown in **Figure 6**. The nodes are always evenly spaced along the wave. At points in the standing wave where constructive interference occurs, the amplitude is greater than zero. Points of maximum amplitude on a standing wave are called **antinodes**. The antinodes always occur halfway between two nodes.

FIGURE 6 ·······························

Standing Waves
As the frequency of the standing wave increases, more nodes and antinodes are created.

✏️ **Complete the tasks.**

1. **Identify** In the second box, label the nodes and antinodes.

2. **CHALLENGE** In the third box, draw the next standing wave in the series, and label its nodes and antinodes.

1 Wavelength

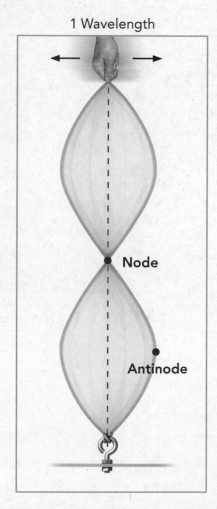

Node

Antinode

1½ Wavelengths

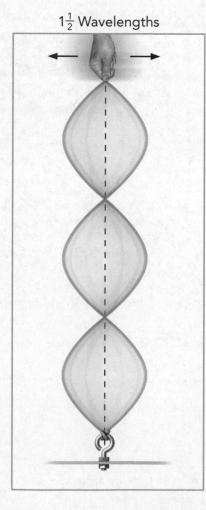

2 Wavelengths

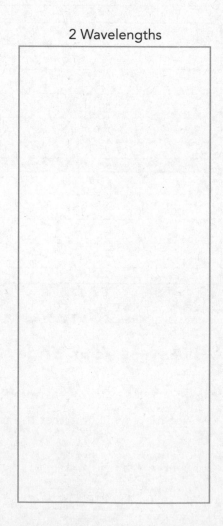

Resonance Have you ever pushed a child on a swing? At first the swing is difficult to push. But once it is going, you need only a gentle push to keep it going. This is because the swing has a natural frequency. Even small pushes that are in rhythm with the swing's natural frequency produce large increases in the swing's amplitude.

Most objects have at least one natural frequency of vibration. Standing waves occur in an object when it vibrates at a natural frequency. If a nearby object vibrates at the same frequency, it can cause resonance. **Resonance** is an increase in the amplitude of a vibration that occurs when external vibrations match an object's natural frequency.

The Tacoma Narrows Bridge, or "Galloping Gertie," may have collapsed because of resonance. Storm winds are said to have resonated with the natural frequency of the bridge. This caused the amplitude of the bridge's sway to increase until the bridge collapsed. You can see the result of the collapse in **Figure 7**.

FIGURE 7 ·····························

The Power of Resonance
Winds blew as fast as 67 km/h during the storm in which the Tacoma Narrows Bridge collapsed.

✏ **Redesign** What might engineers do differently when designing a new bridge for this location?

_____

_____

_____

Lab zone® Do the Quick Lab *Standing Waves.*

🔑 Assess Your Understanding

2a. Describe What causes resonance to occur?

_____

_____

b. ↻ Relate Cause and Effect What causes nodes to form in a standing wave?

_____

_____

got it?

○ **I get it!** Now I know that standing waves form when _____

_____

_____

_____

○ **I need extra help with** _____

Go to my science ⑤ coach *online for help with this subject.*

REVIEW THE BIG ?

The basic properties of waves are _____, _____, _____, and _____.

LESSON 1 What Are Waves?

🔑 Mechanical waves form when a source of energy causes a medium to vibrate.

🔑 The three types of mechanical waves are transverse waves, longitudinal waves, and surface waves.

Vocabulary

- wave • energy • medium • mechanical wave • vibration • transverse wave • crest
- trough • longitudinal wave • compression • rarefaction

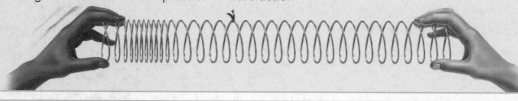

LESSON 2 Properties of Waves

🔑 Amplitude describes how far the medium in a wave moves. Wavelength describes a wave's length, and frequency describes how often it occurs. Speed describes how quickly a wave moves.

🔑 The speed, wavelength, and frequency of a wave are related by a mathematical formula:
Speed = Wavelength × Frequency.

Vocabulary

- amplitude • wavelength • frequency • hertz

LESSON 3 Interactions of Waves

🔑 Waves change direction by reflection, refraction, and diffraction.

🔑 There are two types of interference: constructive and destructive.

🔑 If the incoming wave and reflected wave have just the right frequency, they combine to form a wave that appears to stand still. This wave is called a standing wave.

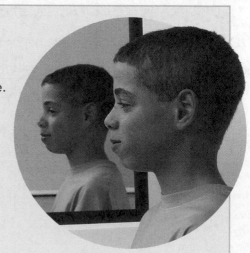

Vocabulary

- reflection • refraction • diffraction • interference
- constructive interference • destructive interference • standing wave
- node • antinode • resonance

Review and Assessment

LESSON 1 What Are Waves?

1. A wave transfers

   a. energy.   **b.** particles

   c. water.   **d.** air.

2. _____ form when a source of energy causes a medium to vibrate.

3. Classify Label the crest(s) and trough(s) on the transverse wave.

4. Compare and Contrast What is the difference between a transverse wave and a longitudinal wave?

_____

_____

_____

_____

_____

_____

5. Relate Cause and Effect Suppose ripples move from one side of a lake to the other. Does the water move across the lake? Explain.

_____

_____

_____

_____

_____

_____

_____

LESSON 2 Properties of Waves

6. The distance between two crests is a wave's

   a. amplitude.   **b.** wavelength.

   c. frequency.   **d.** speed.

7. The _____ of a wave is the number of waves that pass a given point in a certain amount of time.

This wave in the middle of the ocean was produced by an underwater earthquake. Use the diagram to answer Questions 8–10.

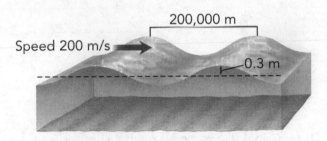

Speed 200 m/s → | 200,000 m | 0.3 m

8. Interpret Diagrams What is the amplitude of the wave? What is its wavelength?

_____

_____

9. Calculate Find the frequency of the wave.

_____

_____

_____

10. math! How long would it take this wave to travel 5,000 km?

_____

_____

_____

_____

LESSON 3 **Interactions of Waves**

11. The bending of a wave due to a change in speed is called

    a. interference.   **b.** reflection.

    c. diffraction.   **d.** refraction.

12. _____ occurs when external vibrations match an object's natural frequency.

13. Predict Two waves are traveling toward each other. The crests from the waves meet. Describe what happens.

_____

_____

_____

_____

_____

14. Draw Conclusions If you push a shopping cart and one wheel hits a rough patch of concrete, it is difficult to steer the cart in a straight line. Explain how this is similar to refraction of a wave as it enters a new medium.

_____

_____

_____

_____

_____

_____

_____

15. Write About It Wave interaction occurs often in the environment. Describe three different ways that you could observe waves changing direction in an indoor swimming pool. Mention as many types of waves as possible.

APPLY THE BIG ? **What are the properties of waves?**

16. During a storm, a TV reporter says, "The ocean waves are 3 meters high. They are about 45 m apart and are hitting the shore every 15 seconds." Think about the four basic properties of waves and describe these ocean waves using the correct science words. (*Hint:* You will need to do some calculations first.)

_____

_____

_____

_____

_____

_____

_____

_____

_____

_____

_____

_____

_____

Standardized Test Prep

Multiple Choice

Circle the letter of the best answer.

1. Two waves approach each other as shown in the diagram below. What will be the amplitude of the wave produced when the crests from each wave meet?

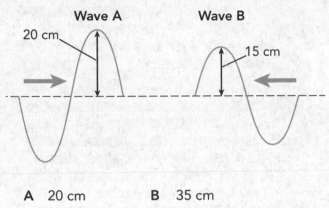

   A 20 cm   **B** 35 cm
   C 15 cm   **D** 5 cm

2. When a wave enters a new medium at 60° and changes speed, the wave

   A does not bend because one side changes speed before the other side.

   B does not bend because the angle is less than 90°.

   C bends because both sides change speed at the same time.

   D bends because one side changes speed before the other side.

3. The speed of a wave in a spring is 3 m/s. If the wavelength is 0.1 m, what is the frequency?

   A 30 Hz   **B** 0.3 Hz
   C 30 m/s   **D** 0.3 m/s

4. Which of the following is true about standing waves?

   A Constructive interference produces points with zero amplitude.

   B The nodes are unevenly spaced along the wave.

   C The amplitude of antinodes is greater than nodes.

   D Nodes are points of maximum energy on the wave.

5. What is the angle of incidence if a reflected wave bounces off a mirror at an angle of 65°?

   A 25°

   B 65°

   C 90°

   D 115°

Constructed Response

Use the diagram and your knowledge of science to help you answer Question 6. Write your answer on a separate sheet of paper.

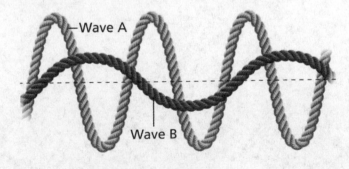

6. The waves shown above travel at the same speed. Which wave has the higher frequency? Which has the longer wavelength? Which has the greater amplitude?

Wall of Water

For as long as humans have sailed on the oceans, ships have disappeared without explanation. People chalked these losses up to bad luck and bad weather. A mysterious phenomenon, proven in 2004 to exist, may finally explain why some large ships are never seen again.

Waves in water usually behave like the other waves around them. Most waves in an area are about the same height and move at the same rate. Ocean waves are rarely more than 15 meters in height and usually form rolling hills of water. But freak monster waves can top 30 meters in height, forming huge walls of water!

Some monster waves form where two currents meet and their waves combine. The weather may be responsible for other monster waves. If an ordinary large wave travels at the same speed and in the same direction as the wind for more than 12 hours, the extra push from the wind can cause the wave to reach monster heights. Some monster waves seem to grow out of normal ocean wave patterns. Physicists theorize that these unstable waves absorb energy from the surrounding waves and grow to vast heights.

Most ships are not designed to withstand 30-meter-high waves, so it's no wonder that little has been found but wreckage. Fortunately, scientists are working on ways to protect ships and sailors in the face of these enormous destructive waves.

Model It Research how so-called monster waves focus and amplify the effects of surrounding waves. Use computer technology to create a diagram or to model the effects. Explain your diagram or model to a classmate.

An Operatic Superpower

Can someone really break a glass by singing a high note? It may seem like a superpower, but the human voice does have the power to shatter a crystal wine glass! This feat is commonly credited to opera singers because they have very powerful and well-trained voices.

Many wine glasses are made of a type of glass called crystal. The molecules in a crystal glass are arranged in a repeating pattern that forms a repeating internal structure. If you tap a crystal object, you can hear a clear tone. That tone is the natural resonant frequency of vibration for that crystal. When the crystal is exposed to a sound at that frequency, the molecules of the crystal vibrate. When the glass vibrates too much, the shape of the glass distorts, which causes the glass to crack. The cracks expand very rapidly, and the crystal shatters.

A trained singer can reproduce the natural frequency of a crystal glass. If the singer can sing the tone of the crystal's natural frequency loudly enough, the singing can shatter the glass!

Design It Resonant frequencies can also be used to make music. Glass harps use wine glasses filled with varying amounts of water to create different notes. The player runs a moistened finger around the rim of each glass. The size of the glass and the amount of water determine which note sounds. Research to learn more about how glass harps work. Then design an experiment to test the amount of water needed to create different pitches. Create a one-page procedure for your experiment.

HOW DOES MUSIC TRAVEL TO YOUR EARS?

THE BIG

What determines the pitch and loudness of sound?

As these New Orleans musicians play their instruments, vibrations travel through the air as sound waves. The audience hears the music when their ears detect the sound waves. **⚠ Infer How do you hear sound from a drum?**

> UNTAMED SCIENCE Watch the **Untamed Science** video to learn more about sound.

_____

_____

_____

_____

_____

_____

_____

Sound

2 Getting Started

Check Your Understanding

1. Background Read the paragraph below and then answer the question.

One morning, an earthquake occurs in California. The ground **vibrates** as **waves** travel out in all directions from the source of the earthquake. The rocks inside Earth are the **medium** that transmits the waves.

> To **vibrate** is to move back and forth.
>
> **Waves** are disturbances that carry energy from one place to another.
>
> A **medium** is a material through which a wave travels.

• What happens inside Earth during an earthquake?

_____

_____

> **MY READING WEB** If you had trouble completing the question above, visit **My Reading Web** and type in *Sound*.

Vocabulary Skill

Identify Multiple Meanings Some familiar words have more than one meaning. Words you use every day may have different meanings in science. Look at the different meanings of the words below.

Word	Everyday Meaning	Scientific Meaning
medium	*adj.* in the middle in quality, amount, or size **Example:** The boy is *medium* in size and build.	*n.* the material through which a wave travels **Example:** Air is a common *medium* for sound to travel through.
reflect	*v.* to express or show **Example:** Her skills in basketball *reflect* years of training.	*v.* to be bent or thrown back **Example:** The water waves *reflect* off the sides of the pool.

2. Quick Check Circle the sentence below that uses the scientific meaning of the word *reflect*.

• Her article *reflects* thorough research.

• Light waves *reflect* off the surface of a mirror.

density

pitch

decibel

intensity

Chapter Preview

LESSON 1
- density
  - ↻ Identify the Main Idea
  - △ Graph

LESSON 2
- pitch
- loudness
- intensity
- decibel
- Doppler effect
  - ↻ Compare and Contrast
  - △ Make Models

LESSON 3
- music
- fundamental tone
- overtone
  - ↻ Identify Supporting Evidence
  - △ Predict

LESSON 4
- ear canal
- eardrum
- cochlea
  - ↻ Relate Cause and Effect
  - △ Observe

LESSON 5
- echolocation
- ultrasound
- sonar
- sonogram
  - ↻ Ask Questions
  - △ Calculate

▷ **VOCAB FLASH CARDS** For extra help with vocabulary, visit **Vocab Flash Cards** and type in *Sound.*

The Nature of Sound

🔑 **What Is Sound?**

🔑 **What Factors Affect the Speed of Sound?**

my planet Diary

FUN FACTS

Thunder and Lightning

It's a hot, sticky summer day, and the sky is filled with dark clouds. Suddenly, a flash of light zigzags through the air! A few seconds later, you hear the loud crack of thunder.

The lightning you see causes the thunder you hear. The reason you see lightning before you hear thunder is because light travels much faster than sound. You can use this fact to figure out how close the storm is. After you see a flash of lightning, count off the seconds until you hear the thunder. Divide the number of seconds by five. The result gives the approximate distance (in miles) to the storm.

Write your answer to the question below.
You notice that the time between seeing the lightning and hearing the thunder is increasing. What does this mean?

_____

_____

_____

_____

▶ **PLANET DIARY** Go to **Planet Diary** to learn more about the nature of sound.

Lab zone® Do the Inquiry Warm-Up *What Is Sound?*

What Is Sound?

Here is a riddle: If a tree falls in a forest and no one hears it, does the tree make a sound? To a scientist, a falling tree makes a sound whether someone hears it or not. When a tree falls, the energy with which it strikes the ground causes a disturbance. Particles in the ground and the air begin to vibrate, or move back and forth. The vibrations create a sound wave as the energy travels through two mediums—air and the ground. 🔑 **Sound is a disturbance that travels through a medium as a longitudinal wave.**

Vocabulary
- density

Skills
↻ Reading: Identify the Main Idea
△ Inquiry: Graph

Making Sound Waves

A sound wave begins with a vibration. Look at the drum shown in **Figure 1.** When the side of the drum (called the drumhead) is struck, it vibrates rapidly in and out. These vibrations disturb nearby air particles. Each time the drumhead moves outward, it pushes air particles together, creating a *compression*. When the drumhead moves inward, the air particles bounce back and spread out, creating a *rarefaction*. These compressions and rarefactions travel through the air as longitudinal waves.

How Sound Waves Travel

Like other mechanical waves, sound waves carry energy through a medium without moving the particles of the medium along. Each particle of the medium vibrates as the disturbance passes. When the disturbance reaches your ears, you hear the sound.

A common medium for sound is air. But sound can travel through solids and liquids, too. For example, when you knock on a solid wooden door, the particles in the wood vibrate. The vibrations make sound waves that travel through the door. When the waves reach the other side of the door, they make sound waves in the air.

Vocabulary Identify Multiple Meanings Review the multiple meanings of the words in the Getting Started section and answer the question. What is the material through which sound waves travel?

_____

FIGURE 1 ·······················
Sound Waves
As the drumheads vibrate, they create sound waves that travel through the air.

✏ **Interpret Diagrams** Label each box as a compression or a rarefaction. Explain how you knew what to label them.

_____

_____

_____

Wavelength

FIGURE 2 ·

Diffraction

Diffraction occurs when sound waves pass through an opening such as a doorway.

✎ **Identify** Which diagram— A, B, or C—correctly shows what happens to sound waves when they pass through the doorway? Explain your answer.

_____

_____

_____

_____

_____

_____

_____

_____

_____

Diffraction of Sound Waves

Have you ever wondered why when you are sitting in a classroom you can hear your friends talking in the hallway before they walk through the doorway? You hear them because sound waves do not always travel in straight lines. Sound waves can diffract, or bend, around the edges of an opening, such as a doorway.

Sound waves can also diffract around obstacles or corners. This is why you can hear someone who is talking in the hallway before the person walks around the corner. The sound waves bend around the corner. Then they spread out so you can hear them even though you cannot see who is talking. Remember this the next time you want to tell a secret!

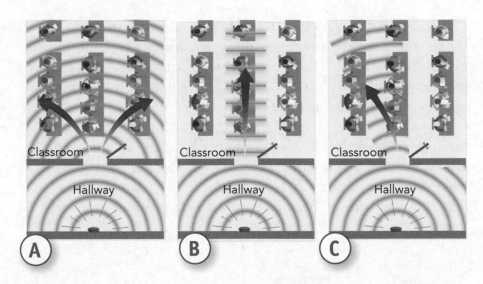

Lab zone® Do the Quick Lab
Understanding Sound.

🔑 Assess Your Understanding

1a. Identify A sound wave carries _____ through a medium.

b. Compare and Contrast In a sound wave, the particles in the medium are close together in a (compression/rarefaction) and farther apart in a (compression/rarefaction).

c. Apply Concepts Explain why you can hear a ringing telephone through a closed door.

_____

_____

_____

_____

got it? ·

○ **I get it!** Now I know sound is _____

_____

○ **I need extra help with** _____

Go to **MY SCIENCE COACH** online for help with this subject.

What Factors Affect the Speed of Sound?

Suppose you were in a stadium watching the baseball player in **Figure 3.** You might see the bat hit the ball before you hear the hit. It is possible to see an action before you hear it because sound travels much more slowly than light. At room temperature, about 20°C, sound travels through air at 342 m/s. This is nearly 900,000 times slower than the speed of light! But the speed of sound is not always 342 m/s. Sound waves travel at different speeds in different media. **The speed of sound depends on the temperature, stiffness, and density of the medium the sound travels through.**

Temperature In a given liquid or gas, sound travels more slowly at lower temperatures than at higher temperatures. Why? At lower temperatures, the particles of a medium move more slowly than at higher temperatures. It is more difficult for the particles to move, and they return to their original positions more slowly.

FIGURE 3 ··

Speed of Sound in Air

How fast the sound of the bat hitting the ball travels depends on the air temperature. The data in the table show how the speed of sound in air changes with temperature.

✏ **Use the data to answer the questions.**

1. **Graph** Create a line graph. Plot temperature on the horizontal axis and speed on the vertical axis. Give the graph a title.

2. **Predict** What might the speed of sound be at 30°C? _____

Air Temperature (°C)	Speed (m/s)
−20	318
−10	324
0	330
10	336
20	342

37

Stiffness Years ago, Native Americans put their ears to the ground to find out if herds of bison or other animals were nearby. By listening for sounds in the ground they could hear the herds sooner than if they listened for sounds in the air. What is it about the state of the medium—solid, liquid, or gas—that determines the speed of sound?

The speed of sound depends on the stiffness of the medium. Sound travels more quickly in stiff media because when the particles of the medium are compressed, they quickly spread out again. For example, steel is stiffer than wood. If you knocked on both a wooden and steel door of the same thickness, the steel door would transmit the sound more easily. Sound also travels better over long distances in stiff media because sound waves lose energy more slowly than in less stiff media.

Solids are stiffer than liquids or gases. The particles in a solid are close together, so they bounce back and forth quickly as the compressions and rarefactions of the sound waves pass by. Most liquids are not as stiff as solids. So sound does not travel as fast in liquids as it does in solids. Gases are not very stiff. Sound generally travels the slowest in gases.

do the math! Analyzing Data

The table shows the speed of sound in different media. Use the data to answer the following questions.

❶ **Interpret Tables** In general, does sound travel faster in solids, liquids, or gases?

_____

❷ **Infer** Which substance is stiffer—air or water?

_____

❸ **Infer** What is the stiffest substance in the table?

_____

❹ **Apply Concepts** Suppose you put your ear to a steel fence. You tell your friend to yell and tap the fence at the same time from far away. Which do you think that you will hear first, the yell or the tap? Why?

_____

_____

_____

_____

_____

❺ CHALLENGE How many times faster does sound travel in a diamond than in air?

_____

Speed of Sound	
Medium	Speed (m/s)
Gases (20°C)	
Air	342
Helium	977
Liquids (20°C)	
Mercury	1,450
Fresh water	1,482
Solids	
Lead	1,200
Plastic	1,800
Hardwood	4,000
Steel	5,200
Diamond	12,000

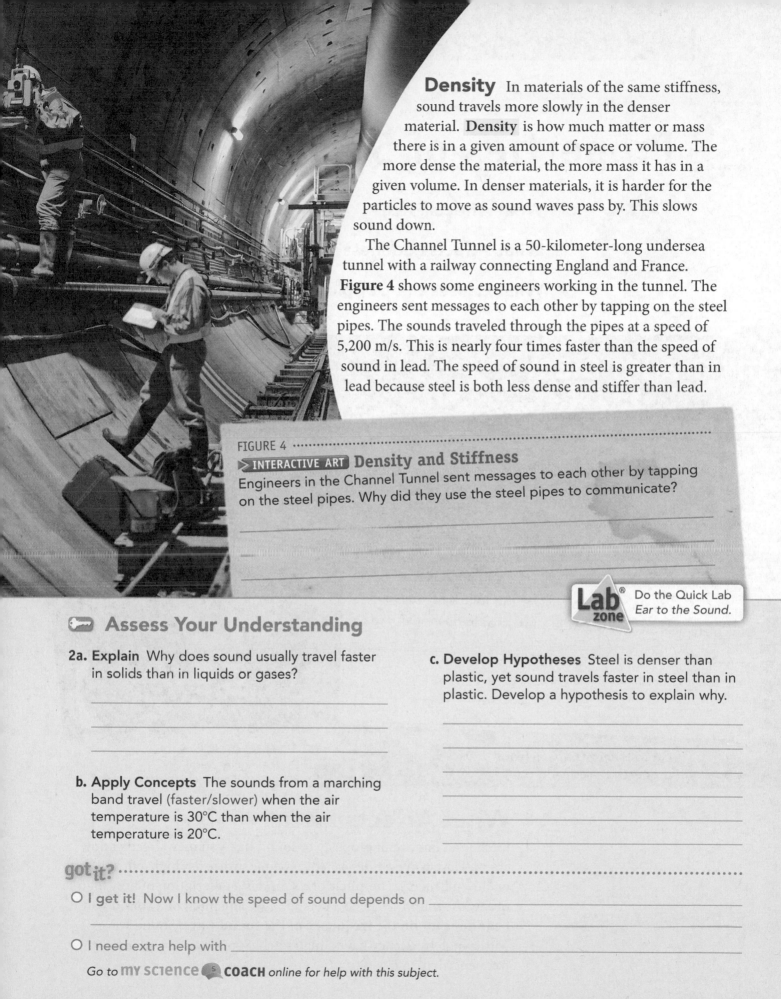

Density In materials of the same stiffness, sound travels more slowly in the denser material. **Density** is how much matter or mass there is in a given amount of space or volume. The more dense the material, the more mass it has in a given volume. In denser materials, it is harder for the particles to move as sound waves pass by. This slows sound down.

The Channel Tunnel is a 50-kilometer-long undersea tunnel with a railway connecting England and France. **Figure 4** shows some engineers working in the tunnel. The engineers sent messages to each other by tapping on the steel pipes. The sounds traveled through the pipes at a speed of 5,200 m/s. This is nearly four times faster than the speed of sound in lead. The speed of sound in steel is greater than in lead because steel is both less dense and stiffer than lead.

FIGURE 4 ··

> **INTERACTIVE ART** **Density and Stiffness**
Engineers in the Channel Tunnel sent messages to each other by tapping on the steel pipes. Why did they use the steel pipes to communicate?

_____

_____

_____

Lab ® Do the Quick Lab
zone *Ear to the Sound.*

Assess Your Understanding

2a. Explain Why does sound usually travel faster in solids than in liquids or gases?

_____

_____

_____

b. Apply Concepts The sounds from a marching band travel (faster/slower) when the air temperature is 30°C than when the air temperature is 20°C.

c. Develop Hypotheses Steel is denser than plastic, yet sound travels faster in steel than in plastic. Develop a hypothesis to explain why.

_____

_____

_____

_____

_____

_____

_____

got it? ···

○ **I get it!** Now I know the speed of sound depends on _____

_____

○ **I need extra help with** _____

Go to **MY SCIENCE COACH** online for help with this subject.

Properties of Sound

🔑 **What Affects Pitch?**

🔑 **What Affects Loudness?**

🔑 **What Causes the Doppler Effect?**

my PLANET DiaRY

Silent Call

To get a dog's attention, a dog trainer blows into a small whistle. But you don't hear a thing. Dogs can hear frequencies well above the human range of hearing. Frequency is measured in hertz (Hz), or the number of sound waves a vibrating object gives off per second. A higher frequency means that the sound has a higher pitch. The table compares the range of frequencies that humans and various animals can hear.

Use the data in the table to answer the following question.

Which animal can hear the widest range of frequencies?

_____

_____

_____

▶ **PLANET DIARY** Go to **Planet Diary** to learn more about the properties of sound.

SCIENCE STATS

Animal	Range of Hearing (in Hertz)
Human	20–20,000
Dog	67–45,000
Mouse	1,000–91,000
Cat	45–64,000
Bullfrog	100–2,500
Elephant	16–12,000

 Lab zone® Do the Inquiry Warm-Up *How Does Amplitude Affect Loudness?*

What Affects Pitch?

Pitch is an important property of sound that you may already know about. Have you ever described someone's voice as "high-pitched" or "low-pitched"? The **pitch** of a sound is a description of how high or low the sound seems to a person. 🔑 **The pitch of a sound you hear depends on the frequency of the sound wave.** Sound waves with a high frequency have a high pitch. Sound waves with a low frequency have a low pitch.

Vocabulary

- pitch • loudness • intensity • decibel
- Doppler effect

Skills

- ⟳ Reading: Compare and Contrast
- △ Inquiry: Make Models

The frequency of a sound wave depends on how fast the source of the sound is vibrating. For example, when you speak or sing, air from your lungs rushes past your vocal cords, making them vibrate. This produces sound waves. To sing specific pitches, or notes, you use muscles in your throat to stretch or relax your vocal cords. When your vocal cords stretch, they vibrate more quickly as the air rushes by them. This creates higher-frequency sound waves that have higher pitches. When your vocal cords relax, lower-frequency sound waves with lower pitches are produced.

Frequency is measured in hertz (Hz). For example, a frequency of 50 Hz means 50 vibrations per second. A trained soprano voice can produce frequencies higher than 1,000 Hz. A bass singer can produce frequencies lower than 80 Hz. Young people can normally hear sounds with frequencies between 20 Hz and 20,000 Hz.

FIGURE 1 ·····································

Pitch

The female soprano singer sings high notes and the male bass singer sings low notes.

△ **Make Models** In the bubble above the bass singer, draw lines to represent the frequency of the sound wave for a low note. Then explain your drawing.

_____

_____

_____

Lab zone® Do the Lab Investigation *Changing Pitch.*

⊶ Assess Your Understanding

got it? ··

○ I get it! Now I know the pitch of a sound that you hear depends on_____

_____

○ I need extra help with _____

Go to my science ⓢ coach *online for help with this subject.*

What Affects Loudness?

Loudness is another important property of sound. You probably already know about loudness. For example, the closer you are to a sound, the louder it is. Also, a whisper in your ear can be just as loud as a shout from a block away. **Loudness** describes your awareness of the energy of a sound. 🔑 **The loudness of a sound depends on the energy and intensity of the sound wave.**

Energy If you hit a drum lightly, you hear a sound. If you hit the drum harder, you hear a louder sound. Why? When you hit a drum harder, you transfer more energy to it. This causes the amplitude, or the distance the drumhead moves from its rest position, to increase. A sound source vibrating with a large amplitude produces a sound wave with a large amplitude. Recall that the greater the amplitude of a wave, the more energy it has. So the more energy a sound wave has, the louder it sounds.

Intensity If you were to move closer to the stage shown in **Figure 2,** the voices of the performers would sound louder. Why? Close to the sound source, a sound wave covers a small area. As a wave travels away from the source, it covers more area. The total energy of the wave, however, stays the same. Therefore, the closer a sound wave is to its source, the more energy it has in a given area. The amount of energy a sound wave carries per second through a unit area is its **intensity.** A sound wave of greater intensity sounds louder.

FIGURE 2 ·······································

Intensity

Sound waves spread out as they travel away from the source.

✏️ **Interpret Diagrams** Rank the intensity of a sound wave at the three locations. A ranking of 1 is the greatest. Write your answers in the boxes. Explain your answers.

_____

_____

_____

_____

_____

_____

Measuring Loudness The loudness of different sounds is compared using a unit called the **decibel** (dB). The table in the Apply It below compares the loudness of some familiar sounds. The loudness of a sound you can barely hear is about 0 dB. A 10-dB increase in loudness represents a tenfold increase in the intensity of the sound. For example, a 10-dB sound is ten times more intense than a 0-dB sound. A 20-dB sound is 100 times more intense than a 0-dB sound and ten times more intense than a 10-dB sound. Sounds louder than 100 dB can cause damage to your ears, especially if you listen to those sounds for long periods of time. For this reason, airport workers, like the one shown to the right, wear hearing protection.

apply it!

Use the table to answer the questions.

❶ Which sounds louder, a rock concert or a jet plane at takeoff?_____

❷ Which sounds could be dangerous to your ears?

_____

_____

❸ **Calculate** How much more intense is a 20-dB whisper than the threshold of human hearing?

_____

❹ **CHALLENGE** How much more intense is a 90-dB hair dryer than 60-dB street traffic?

_____

Measuring Loudness	
Sound	**Loudness (dB)**
Threshold of human hearing	0
Whisper	15–20
Normal conversation	40–50
Busy street traffic	60–70
Hairdryer	80–90
Rock concert	110–120
Headphones at peak volume	120
Jet plane at takeoff	120–160

Do the Quick Lab
Listen to This.

🔑 Assess Your Understanding

1a. Review The amount of energy a sound wave carries per second through a unit area is its

_____

b. Describe The intensity of a sound wave (increases/decreases) with distance.

c. Calculate An 80-dB sound is _____ times more intense than a 60-dB sound.

got it?

○ I get it! Now I know that the loudness of a sound depends on _____

_____

○ I need extra help with _____

Go to **my science** ⑤ **coach** *online for help with this subject.*

What Causes the Doppler Effect?

Have you ever listened to the siren of a firetruck on its way to a fire? If so, then you probably noticed that as the truck goes by, the pitch of the siren drops. But the pitch of the siren stays constant for the firefighters in the truck. The siren's pitch changes only if it is moving toward or away from a listener.

The change in frequency of a wave as its source moves in relation to an observer is called the **Doppler effect.** If the waves are sound waves, the change in frequency is heard as a change in pitch. The Doppler effect is named after the Austrian scientist Christian Doppler (1803–1853). **The Doppler effect occurs because the motion of the source causes the waves to either get closer together or spread out.**

Figure 3 shows how sound waves from a moving source behave. Each time the siren sends out a new wave, the firetruck moves ahead in the same direction as the waves in front of the truck. This causes the waves to get closer together. Because the waves are closer together, they have a shorter wavelength and a higher frequency as they reach observers in front of the truck. As the truck moves away, it travels in the opposite direction of the sound waves behind it. This causes the waves to spread out. Because they spread out, the waves have a longer wavelength and a lower frequency as they reach the observers behind the truck.

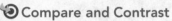

↻Compare and Contrast
The waves in front of a moving sound source have a (shorter/longer) wavelength. The waves behind a moving sound source have a (shorter/longer) wavelength.

FIGURE 3 ·····································

> **ART IN MOTION** **The Doppler Effect**
As the firetruck speeds by, observers hear a change in the pitch of the siren. ✏ **Identify** Circle the answer that describes the pitch that the observers hear.

People behind the firetruck hear a (lower/higher) pitch than the firefighters in the truck hear.

People standing in front of the firetruck hear a (lower/higher) pitch than the firefighters in the truck hear.

FIRE DEPARTMENT

EXPLORE THE BIG

How Your Headphones Work

What determines the pitch and loudness of sound?

FIGURE 4 ·····································

> INTERACTIVE ART Headphones turn an electrical signal into sound waves.

1 An electrical signal travels up a wire.

2 The electrical signal causes a magnet to vibrate.

3 The magnet is attached to a thin cone of material. The vibrating cone sends sound waves through the air.

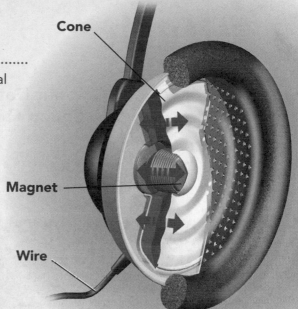

Cone

Magnet

Wire

> **Compare and Contrast** Compare how a drum and headphones produce sounds of higher pitch and greater loudness.

_____

_____

_____

_____

_____

_____

Lab zone® Do the Quick Lab *Pipe Sounds.*

 Assess Your Understanding

2. ANSWER THE BIG ? What determines the pitch and loudness of sound?

_____

_____

_____

_____

_____

got it?

○ **I get it!** Now I know that the Doppler effect occurs because _____

_____

_____

○ I need extra help with _____

Go to my science COACH *online for help with this subject.*

Music

UNLOCK
THE BIG
?

🔑 **What Determines
Sound Quality?**

MY PLANET DIARY

Posted by: Jameel

Location: Orlando, Florida

I play an instrument called the French horn. The French horn has valves, a bell, a mouthpiece, and three keys. It is interesting how pitch affects the music that I make. While I was practicing, the music sounded out of tune. I realized I hadn't tuned the instrument, so I slid the tuning valve up and down until I got the right pitch. I like to play my instrument because it enhances my hand/eye coordination. I also love the sound of the music when I play it right.

Write your answers to the questions below.

1. What does it mean to tune an instrument?

_____

_____

_____

2. The musicians in a marching band do not tune their instruments until they are outside. Why do you suppose this is?

_____

_____

▶ PLANET DIARY Go to **Planet Diary** to learn more about music.

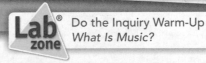

Do the Inquiry Warm-Up
What Is Music?

What Determines Sound Quality?

Most people agree on what is and what is not music. **Music** is a set of notes that combine in patterns that are pleasing. Noise, on the other hand, usually has no pleasing patterns. When you describe a sound as pleasant or unpleasant, you are describing sound quality. The sound quality of music depends on the instruments making the music. 🔑 **The sound quality of musical instruments results from blending a fundamental tone with its overtones.**

Vocabulary
- music • fundamental tone
- overtone

Skills
- ⟳ Reading: Identify Supporting Evidence
- △ Inquiry: Predict

Fundamental Tones and Overtones To understand sound quality, consider the example of a guitar string. As the string vibrates, waves travel along the string and reflect back, setting up a standing wave. Standing waves occur in all musical instruments when they are played. In a trumpet, for example, standing waves occur in a vibrating column of air. In a drum, standing waves occur in a vibrating drumhead.

A standing wave can occur only at specific frequencies, which are called natural frequencies. The lowest natural frequency is called the **fundamental tone.** The higher natural frequencies are called overtones. **Overtones** have frequencies that are two, three, or more times the frequency of the fundamental tone.

Most instruments produce several natural frequencies at once. The fundamental tone determines what note you hear. For example, when a guitar and a trumpet play middle C, they both produce a fundamental tone of 262 Hz. Each instrument produces different overtones, so the blending of the fundamental tones and overtones produces different sound qualities. The size, shape, and material of the instrument determine which overtones are loudest.

⟳ **Identify Supporting Evidence** Underline the reason that the sound quality of a guitar is different from that of a trumpet.

it!

A guitar can produce a fundamental tone of 262 Hz. The diagrams show how the fundamental tone and the first two overtones combine to produce the unique sound for a guitar string.

❶ Calculate What are the frequencies of the first and second overtones?

Frequency of first overtone = _____

Frequency of second overtone = _____

❷ Explain What determines which overtone will be loudest?

_____

_____

❸ CHALLENGE Which overtone will be loudest? Why?

_____

_____

Fundamental tone

+

First overtone

+

Second overtone

=

Resulting sound wave

Groups of Musical Instruments

How does a musician control the sounds produced by a musical instrument? To control pitch, the musician changes the fundamental tones. To control loudness, the musician changes the energy of the vibrations. The way pitch and loudness are controlled varies among the groups of instruments.

Stringed Instruments

Stringed instruments include the guitar, violin, cello, and double bass. The strings of these instruments produce sound by vibrating when they are plucked or rubbed with a bow. To create louder sounds, the musicians pluck the strings harder or press the bow harder against the strings. To vary the pitch, the musicians change the length of the vibrating string. They do this by placing their fingers on different places along the string as they play. A short string produces a higher-pitched sound than a long string. The material, thickness, and tightness of a string also affect the pitch it produces.

FIGURE 1 ···

Violin

The musician creates sound by rubbing the bow across the strings.

✎ **Interpret Photos** Insert an arrow in the box above to indicate in what direction the musician should move his finger to create a higher-pitched sound.

Percussion Instruments

Percussion instruments include the drums, bells, cymbals, and xylophone. These instruments vibrate when struck. To create louder sounds, the musician hits the instrument harder. The pitch of these instruments depends on the material from which they are made, the size of the instrument, and the part of the instrument that is played. For example, a large drum produces a lower pitch than a small drum.

FIGURE 2 ···

Drums

The musicians create sound by hitting the drums.

✎ **Identify** Circle the drum that would produce the highest pitch.

Wind Instruments

Wind instruments include the trumpet, trombone, clarinet, and flute. These instruments create sound when the musician blows on or across the mouthpiece. This causes the air column inside the instrument to vibrate. The musician creates a louder sound by blowing harder. The musician changes pitch by changing the length of the air column. A shorter air column produces a higher pitch than a longer air column. In many wind instruments, the musician changes the length of the air column by pressing keys or valves. In the trombone, the musician changes the length of the air column by moving a slide either closer to or farther away from the mouthpiece.

FIGURE 3 ·······························

Trombone

The musician creates sound by blowing into the mouthpiece.

Predict If the musician pushes the slide away from her, what will happen to the pitch of the trombone? Why?

_____

_____

_____

_____

Slide

Lab zone Do the Quick Lab *How Can You Change Pitch?*

🔑 Assess Your Understanding

1a. List What are the three groups of musical instruments?

_____

b. Classify What types of instruments are a bell, a whistle, and a banjo?

_____

_____

_____

got it?

○ **I get it!** Now I know the sound quality of a musical instrument results from _____

_____

_____

○ **I need extra help with** _____

Go to **MY SCIENCE COACH** online for help with this subject.

UNLOCK THE BIG Q?

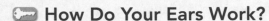 How Do Your Ears Work?

my planet Diary

MISCONCEPTION

Misconception: Deaf people are not able to sense music.

Did you know that Beethoven composed many great works after he lost his hearing? Like all musicians, Beethoven could read music and hear it being played in his mind. But Beethoven may have been able to appreciate music in ways that musicians with normal hearing cannot. A recent study has shown that deaf people can sense vibrations in the same area of the brain that is used to hear. These vibrations create a pattern that they recognize and enjoy.

Deaf musicians can also feel vibrations in different parts of their bodies. The famous solo percussionist Evelyn Glennie performs barefoot so that she can better feel the vibrations in the floor. She also notices changes in the density of the air around her.

Write your answers to the questions below.

1. What senses are used to feel music?

_____

2. Describe an example of how you have felt the vibrations from music.

_____

_____

_____

> PLANET DIARY Go to **Planet Diary** to learn more about hearing sound.

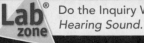 Do the Inquiry Warm-Up *Hearing Sound.*

Vocabulary
- ear canal
- eardrum
- cochlea

Skills
↻ Reading: Relate Cause and Effect
△ Inquiry: Observe

How Do Your Ears Work?

The library is quiet. You are doing your homework. Suddenly, a door slams shut. Startled, you turn in the direction of the sound. Your ears detected the sound waves produced by the slamming door. But how exactly did your brain receive the information?

🗝 **Your ear gathers sound waves and sends information about sound to your brain.** Your ear has three main sections: the outer ear, the middle ear, and the inner ear. Each section has a different function. The outer ear funnels sound waves, the middle ear transmits the waves inward, and the inner ear converts sound waves into a form that travels to your brain.

apply it!

One of the functions of your ears is to locate the direction of sounds.

❶ Ask your partner to sit in a chair with eyes closed.

❷ △Observe Tap two pencils together in different locations around your partner's head and face. Ask your partner to identify what direction the sounds come from. Record the locations where the taps are easily identified. Record the locations where the taps are harder to identify.

_____

_____

_____

_____

_____

_____

❸ Switch places with your partner and repeat steps 1 and 2.

❹ **Draw Conclusions** Discuss which sounds were easily located. Suggest an explanation for your observations.

_____

_____

_____

_____

_____

_____

_____

_____

_____

_____

_____

51

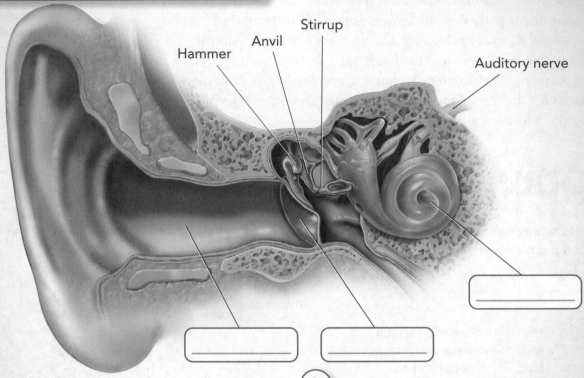

1 Outer Ear

The first section of your ear is the outer ear. The outermost part of your outer ear looks and acts like a funnel. It collects sound waves and directs them into a narrow region called the **ear canal.** Your ear canal is a few centimeters long and ends at the eardrum. The **eardrum** is a small, tightly stretched, drumlike membrane. The sound waves make your eardrum vibrate, just as a drum vibrates when you strike it.

2 Middle Ear

Behind the eardrum is the middle ear. The middle ear contains the three smallest bones in your body—the hammer, the anvil, and the stirrup. The hammer is attached to the eardrum. When the eardrum vibrates, the hammer does too. The hammer then transmits vibrations first to the anvil and then to the stirrup.

Hammer

Anvil

Stirrup

Auditory nerve

FIGURE 1 ···

The Human Ear

The ear has three main sections: the outer ear, the middle ear, and the inner ear.

✎ **Answer the following questions.**

1. **Name** Label the ear canal, eardrum, and cochlea.

2. **Identify** Circle each section of the ear. Draw a line from each circle to its matching text box.

3. **CHALLENGE** Which structure provides evidence that sound can travel through liquids? Explain.

_____

_____

_____

_____

3 Inner Ear

A membrane separates the middle ear from the inner ear, the third section of the ear. When the stirrup vibrates against this membrane, the vibrations pass into the cochlea. The **cochlea** (KAHK lee uh) is a liquid-filled cavity shaped like a snail shell. The cochlea contains more than 10,000 tiny structures called hair cells. These hair cells have hairlike projections that float in the liquid of the cochlea. When vibrations move through the liquid, the hair cells move, causing messages to be sent to the brain through the auditory nerve. The brain processes these messages and tells you that you've heard sound.

Hearing Loss
When hearing loss occurs, a person may have difficulty hearing soft sounds or high-pitched sounds. Hearing loss can occur suddenly if the eardrum is damaged or punctured. (Imagine trying to play a torn drum!) For this reason, it is dangerous to put objects into your ear, even to clean it. Hearing loss can also occur gradually. As a person gets older, some hair cells in the cochlea die and do not grow back. People with this kind of hearing loss often have difficulty hearing high-frequency sounds. Extended exposure to loud sounds can also damage hair cells.

For some types of hearing loss, hearing aids can restore some ability to hear. Some hearing aids amplify sounds entering the ear. Others can amplify specific frequencies that a person has lost the ability to hear. For severe forms of hearing loss, a cochlear implant replaces the entire function of the ear. A cochlear implant contains a sound processor, an implant, and electrodes, as shown in **Figure 2**. The sound processor turns sound waves into an electrical signal. The implant transmits the signal to the electrodes. The electrodes stimulate the auditory nerve directly instead of the damaged cochlea.

✎ **Relate Cause and Effect**
Underline three causes of hearing loss.

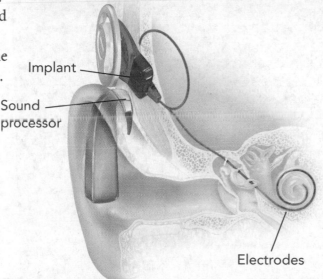

Implant

Sound processor

Electrodes

FIGURE 2 ·······························

A Cochlear Implant
A cochlear implant can restore the ability to hear.

✎ **Explain** How does a cochlear implant replace the function of the ear?

_____

_____

_____

_____

Lab ® Do the Quick Lab *Design and*
zone *Build Hearing Protectors.*

🔑 Assess Your Understanding

1a. List What are the three sections of the ear?

_____

_____

b. Interpret Diagrams What happens to a sound wave as it enters your ear canal?

_____

_____

got it?

○ I get it! Now I know the function of your ear is

_____

_____

_____

○ I need extra help with _____

Go to MY SCIENCE Ⓢ COACH *online for help with this subject.*

5 Using Sound

 **UNLOCK THE BIG Q?**

🔑 **How Do Animals and People Use Sound?**

MY PLANET DIARY

CAREERS

Marine Scientist

Why are marine scientists in Sarasota Bay, Florida, spying on dolphins? Dolphins send out a series of high-frequency clicks to navigate and find food. They whistle to communicate with each other. The scientists are recording underwater sounds in the bay. They are also noting dolphin sightings. They will use the data to determine how boat noise in the bay affects dolphin behavior.

Boat noise, underwater drilling, and sonar devices used by the military have all been shown to affect dolphins, porpoises, and whales. For this reason, it is a rich area of research for marine scientists.

Write your answer to the question below.

Make Judgments How do you think boat noise could affect the dolphins in the bay?

_____

_____

_____

_____

_____

_____

_____

▶ PLANET DIARY Go to **Planet Diary** to learn more about echolocation and ultrasound technologies.

 Lab zone® Do the Inquiry Warm-Up *How Can You Use Time to Measure Distance?*

How Do Animals and People Use Sound?

Have you ever shouted into a canyon or a cave and then waited for the echo? An echo is a reflected sound wave. When a sound wave hits a surface that it cannot pass through, it may reflect. Some practical uses of sound, including echolocation and ultrasound technologies, are based on the fact that sound reflects off surfaces.

Vocabulary
- echolocation • ultrasound
- sonar • sonogram

Skills
- ⟳ Reading: Ask Questions
- △ Inquiry: Calculate

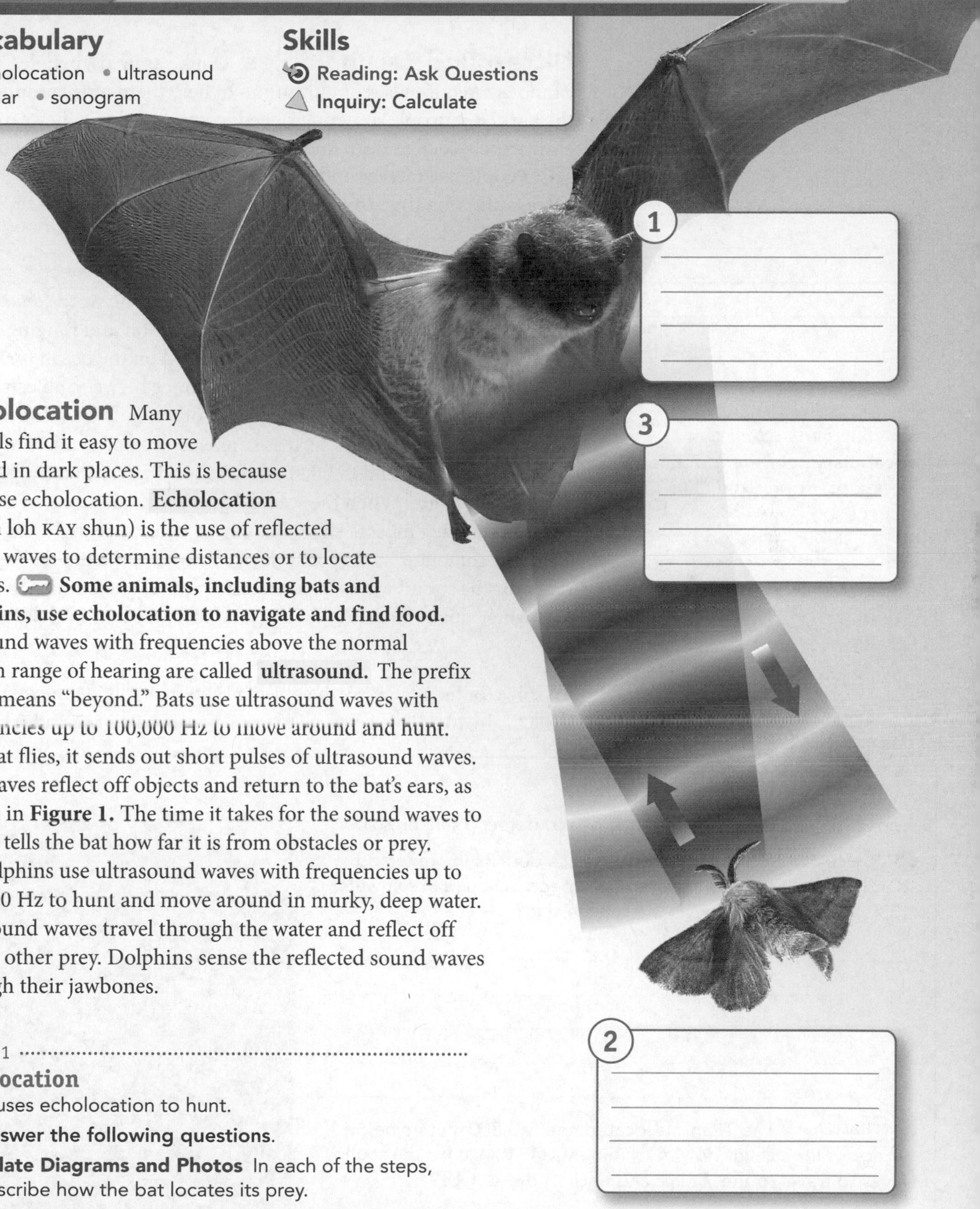

1 _____

3 _____

Echolocation Many animals find it easy to move around in dark places. This is because they use echolocation. **Echolocation** (EK oh loh KAY shun) is the use of reflected sound waves to determine distances or to locate objects. ☞ **Some animals, including bats and dolphins, use echolocation to navigate and find food.**

Sound waves with frequencies above the normal human range of hearing are called **ultrasound.** The prefix *ultra-* means "beyond." Bats use ultrasound waves with frequencies up to 100,000 Hz to move around and hunt. As a bat flies, it sends out short pulses of ultrasound waves. The waves reflect off objects and return to the bat's ears, as shown in **Figure 1.** The time it takes for the sound waves to return tells the bat how far it is from obstacles or prey.

Dolphins use ultrasound waves with frequencies up to 150,000 Hz to hunt and move around in murky, deep water. The sound waves travel through the water and reflect off fish or other prey. Dolphins sense the reflected sound waves through their jawbones.

2 _____

FIGURE 1 ··
Echolocation
A bat uses echolocation to hunt.

✎ **Answer the following questions.**

1. **Relate Diagrams and Photos** In each of the steps, describe how the bat locates its prey.

2. **Explain** Why would the bat have to continue to send out sound waves as it gets closer to its prey?

_____

_____

→ **Ask Questions** Before reading about ultrasound technologies, ask yourself a *What* or *How* question. Then answer your question.

_____

_____

_____

_____

_____

Vocabulary Identify Multiple Meanings Review the multiple meanings of the words in the Getting Started section and complete the sentence. A sonar device detects sound waves after they _____ off objects.

Ultrasound Technologies

Unlike animals, people cannot send out pulses of ultrasound to help them move around in the dark. But people sometimes need to explore places they cannot easily reach, such as deep under water or inside the human body. ☞ **People use ultrasound technologies, such as sonar and ultrasound imaging, to observe things that they cannot see directly.**

Sonar A system that uses reflected sound waves to detect and locate objects under water is called **sonar.** The word *sonar* comes from the initial letters of **so**und **n**avigation **a**nd **r**anging. "Navigation" means finding your way around on the ocean (or in the air). "Ranging" means finding the distance between objects. People use sonar to determine the depth of water, to map the ocean floor, and to locate objects such as sunken ships and schools of fish.

A sonar device sends a burst of ultrasound waves that travel through the water. When the sound waves strike an object or the ocean floor, they reflect. The sonar device detects the reflected waves. A computer in the sonar device measures the time it takes for the sound waves to go out and return. Then it uses the following equation to solve for the total distance that sound travels.

$$\text{Distance} = \text{Speed of sound in water} \times \text{Time}$$

To solve for how far away the object is you must divide the total distance by two. This is because sound waves travel out and return.

apply it!

A sonar device sends out sound waves to detect a sunken ship.

1 Calculate Suppose the sonar device detects the reflected sound waves 10.0 seconds later. The speed of sound in salt water is 1,530 m/s. How far down is the sunken ship?

_____

_____

_____

_____

2 CHALLENGE The *Titanic* is located nearly 3,800 meters below the surface of the ocean. How much time would it take for the sound waves to travel to the *Titanic* and back to the surface?

_____

_____

_____

_____

Ultrasound Imaging Doctors use ultrasound imaging to look inside the human body. An ultrasound imaging device sends ultrasound waves into the body. Then it detects the reflected sound waves. Different parts of the body, such as bones, muscles, the liver, or the heart, reflect sound differently. The device uses the reflected waves to create a picture called a **sonogram**. A doctor can use sonograms to diagnose and treat many medical conditions.

The technician in **Figure 2** is using an ultrasound imaging device to examine a fetus. The technician holds a small probe on the pregnant woman's abdomen. The probe sends out very high frequency ultrasound waves (about 4 million Hz). By analyzing the reflected sound waves, the device builds up a sonogram. The sonogram can show the position of the fetus. Sonograms can also show if there is more than one fetus. In addition to a still picture, ultrasound imaging can produce a video of the fetus.

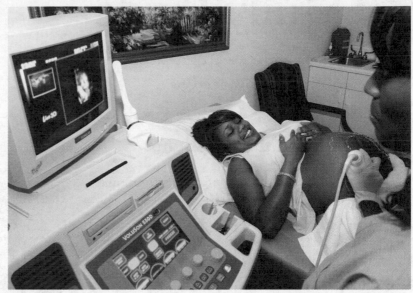

FIGURE 2 ···

> **REAL-WORLD INQUIRY** **Ultrasound in Medicine**

An ultrasound imaging device creates a sonogram of a fetus.

✎ **Explain** How does an ultrasound imaging device work?

_____

_____

_____

_____

_____

Lab ® Do the Quick Lab
zone *Designing Experiments.*

🔑 **Assess Your Understanding**

1a. Define _____ is the use of reflected sound waves to determine distances or to locate objects.

b. Compare and Contrast How is sonar similar to ultrasound imaging? How is it different?

_____

_____

_____

_____

_____

_____

got it?

○ **I get it!** Now I know that animals use

echolocation to _____

_____

_____

and humans use ultrasound technologies to

_____

_____

_____

○ **I need extra help with** _____

Go to **MY SCIENCE** ⬤ **COACH** *online for help with this subject.*

REVIEW THE BIG Q

The pitch of a sound depends on the_____ of the sound wave. The loudness of a sound depends on the _____ and _____ of the sound wave.

LESSON 1 The Nature of Sound

🔑 Sound is a disturbance that travels through a medium as a longitudinal wave.

🔑 The speed of sound depends on the temperature, stiffness, and density of the medium the sound travels through.

Vocabulary
• density

LESSON 2 Properties of Sound

🔑 The pitch of a sound you hear depends on the frequency of the sound wave.

🔑 The loudness of a sound depends on the energy and intensity of the sound wave.

🔑 The Doppler effect occurs because the motion of the source causes the waves to either get closer together or spread out.

Vocabulary
• pitch • loudness • intensity • decibel
• Doppler effect

LESSON 3 Music

🔑 The sound quality of musical instruments results from blending a fundamental tone with its overtones.

Vocabulary
• music
• fundamental tone
• overtone

LESSON 4 Hearing Sound

🔑 Your ear gathers sound waves and sends information about sound to your brain.

Vocabulary
• ear canal
• eardrum
• cochlea

LESSON 5 Using Sound

🔑 Some animals, including bats and dolphins, use echolocation to navigate and find food.

🔑 People use ultrasound technologies, such as sonar and ultrasound imaging, to observe things that they cannot see directly.

Vocabulary
• echolocation
• ultrasound
• sonar
• sonogram

Review and Assessment

LESSON 1 The Nature of Sound

1. What term describes how much matter or mass there is in a given volume?

   a. stiffness   **b.** density

   c. temperature   **d.** diffraction

2. If you increase the temperature of a liquid or gas, a sound wave will travel _____

3. **Summarize** What three properties of a medium affect the speed of sound?

   _____

   _____

4. **Make Models** In the circles below, draw the air particles in a compression and rarefaction of the same sound wave.

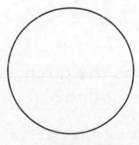 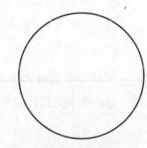

   Compression   Rarefaction

5. **Relate Cause and Effect** Why is a vibration of an object necessary for a sound wave to form?

   _____

   _____

   _____

6. **Infer** Thunder and lightning happen at the same time. Explain why you see the lightning before you hear the thunder.

   _____

   _____

LESSON 2 Properties of Sound

7. What property of sound describes your awareness of the energy of a sound?

   a. loudness   **b.** intensity

   c. pitch   **d.** elasticity

8. As a sound wave travels, its intensity decreases because _____

   _____

9. **Interpret Diagrams** Look at the sound waves coming from the two speakers. Which speaker cone is vibrating faster? How do you know?

   _____

   _____

   _____

10. **Relate Cause and Effect** As a car drives past a person standing on a sidewalk, the driver keeps a hand on the horn. How does the pitch of the horn differ for the driver and the person standing on the sidewalk?

   _____

   _____

   _____

   _____

11. **Write About It** Explain how listening to your headphones at too high a volume can cause just as much damage to your ears as the sounds at a rock concert.

LESSON 3 Music

12. What term describes the lowest natural frequency of the source of a sound?

    a. overtone   **b.** standing wave

    c. fundamental tone   **d.** pitch

13. The quality of sound that a musical instrument produces is the result of _____

_____

_____

14. Apply Concepts A trumpet player pushes down on one of the valves to produce a lower note. How did the length of the air column in the trumpet change? Explain.

_____

_____

_____

_____

LESSON 4 Hearing Sound

15. What part of the ear contains thousands of hair cells that transmit sound?

    a. cochlea   **b.** middle ear

    c. ear canal   **d.** eardrum

16. The middle ear contains the three smallest bones in the body, which are called the

_____, the _____,

and the _____

17. Infer Sometimes a very loud sound or physical contact with an object can tear the eardrum. How would this affect hearing? Why?

_____

_____

_____

_____

LESSON 5 Using Sound

18. What system uses reflected sound waves to detect and locate objects under water?

    a. sonogram   **b.** ultrasound imaging

    c. diffraction   **d.** sonar

19. Some animals use _____

to navigate by sensing reflected sound waves.

20. math! Suppose it takes 6.0 seconds for a sound wave to travel to the bottom of the ocean and back to the surface. If the speed of sound in salt water is 1,530 m/s, how deep is the ocean at this point?

_____

_____

_____

_____

 What determines the pitch and loudness of sound?

21. How could you make sounds of different pitch and loudness with the two drums?

_____

_____

_____

_____

Standardized Test Prep

Multiple Choice

Circle the letter of the best answer.

1. The table below compares the loudness of several different sounds.

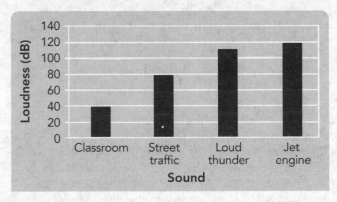

How many times more intense is the sound of a jet engine than the sound of loud thunder?

A 2

B 10

C 20

D 100

2. Fishing boats use sonar to locate schools of fish. What characteristic of sound is most important for this application of sonar?

A Sound waves reflect off some surfaces.

B Sound waves diffract around corners.

C Sound waves interfere when they overlap.

D Sound waves spread out from a source.

3. A trumpet and a piano can both play the same note, but the sound qualities are very different. Why does the sound quality depend on the instrument that produces it?

A Each instrument produces a different fundamental tone.

B Each instrument produces different overtones.

C The amplitude of the notes is different.

D The intensity of the sound is different.

4. Why does sound intensity decrease as the distance from the source increases?

A Most of the energy is absorbed by the particles of the medium.

B The same amount of energy is spread out over a larger area.

C The frequency increases as distance from the source increases.

D The energy of the sound wave decreases.

5. What is the function of the inner ear?

A The inner ear vibrates when sound waves strike it.

B The inner ear converts vibrations into signals that travel to the brain.

C The inner ear increases the frequency of sound waves.

D The inner ear transmits sound waves from the ear canal to the cochlea.

Constructed Response

Use the table below to answer Question 6. Draw your graph on a separate sheet of paper.

6. Create a bar graph to compare highest frequencies heard by and produced by each animal listed. Which animal(s) can produce sounds that are too high for humans to hear?

Animal	Highest Frequency Heard (Hz)	Highest Frequency Produced (Hz)
Human	20,000	1,100
Dog	45,000	1,800
Cat	64,000	1,500
Bat	120,000	120,000
Porpoise	150,000	120,000

CAN YOU HEAR ME NOW?

CRASH! BANG! BEEP BEEP! In cities all across the world, noise pollution is part of everyday life. Noise pollution is loud, distracting sound.

There are many different types of noise pollution. Some of the most common are residential noise, road traffic noise, and air traffic noise. Residential noise pollution occurs in places where people live. It includes noisy neighbors, high-pitched car alarms, and power tools from renovations. Road traffic noise pollution is common at busy intersections or on highways. Helicopters and airplanes cause air traffic noise pollution. Air traffic noise is especially troublesome for people who live or work near airports.

Too much noise can cause hearing loss, lack of sleep, and increased stress. Studies show that students who go to school in areas that have high levels of noise pollution have lower test scores. The noise affects students' ability to concentrate.

More than 100 million Americans are regularly exposed to noise levels higher than 55 decibels—the common standard for background noise levels. As a result, governments are passing laws to reduce noise pollution.

Write About It Write a letter to your town or city council. Identify and explain what the impact of noise pollution is on the people in your town or city. Describe your ideas about how to reduce noise in your area.

NOISY Occupations

Settings and costumes can make a film interesting to watch. But think for a moment about watching a car chase without the sounds of traffic, tires squealing, or motors revving. The scene might look great, but it would be less thrilling.

Several people work to create the sound effects in a movie.

Foley artists create the background noises that make a scene convincing. They create everyday sounds such as footsteps or jingling keys. They also create less ordinary noises, such as punching noises. These noises might not be very obvious, but you would notice if they weren't there.

Sound mixers record all sound effects and dialogue. If all of the sounds were recorded at the same time scenes were filmed, you wouldn't be able to hear a thing the actors were saying—the wrong noises would be loud and cover the speech. So sound mixers record the dialogue and effects separately and mix them together in the studio.

Sound effects editors make sure that everyone follows the sound plan for the film, and that all of the noises happen at the right time in a way that works.

Record It Work in a small group to record an audio track. Design a solution for sounds you have to "fake." For example, how would you make a sound for something dropping from the roof? Play your track for the class—can they tell what is happening?

63

HOW DO SCANS "SEE" YOUR BRAIN?

THE BIG

What kinds of waves make up the electromagnetic spectrum?

It might look like a colorful wig, but this image shows the nerve pathways of the brain. Using machines that read energy from our bodies, doctors can see how and when different areas of the brain are active without surgery or radiation.

When your brain performs a task, such as remembering a phone number, blood circulation to that part of your brain increases. The scan recognizes that activity.

⚠️ **Infer What might the colors of this brain scan mean?**

_____

_____

_____

_____

_____

▷ UNTAMED SCIENCE Watch the **Untamed Science** video to learn more about electromagnetic waves.

Electromagnetic Waves

3 | Getting Started

Check Your Understanding

1. Background Read the paragraph below and then answer the question.

Have you ever stepped in a large puddle? When your foot hits the water, it transfers energy to the water, creating a **wave.** The **medium,** water, **vibrates** with the transfer of energy. The water ripples around your foot.

> A **wave** is a disturbance that transfers energy from place to place.
>
> The material through which a wave travels is the **medium.**
>
> To **vibrate** is to move in a repeated back-and-forth or up-and-down motion.

• What caused the water to vibrate?

_____

_____

> **MY READING WEB** If you had trouble completing the question above, visit **My Reading Web** and type in *Electromagnetic Waves.*

Vocabulary Skill

Greek Word Origins Some science words in this chapter contain word parts with Greek origins. The table below lists some of the Greek words from which the vocabulary words come.

Greek Word	Meaning of Greek Word	Example
mikro-	small	microwaves, *n.* electromagnetic radiation with short wavelengths and high frequencies
-skopion	for seeing or observing	spectroscope, *n.* instrument used to see different colors of light
photos	light	photon, *n.* packet of light energy

2. Quick Check Circle the word part in *spectroscope* that tells you its meaning has to do with viewing.

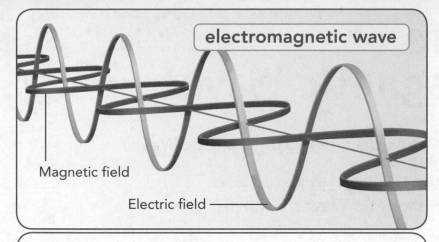

electromagnetic wave

Magnetic field

Electric field

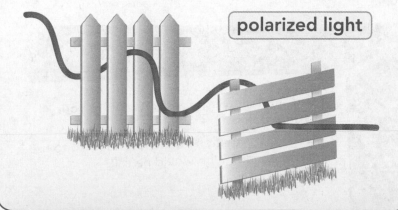

polarized light

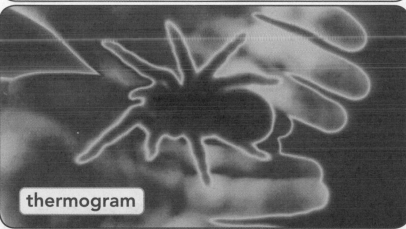

thermogram

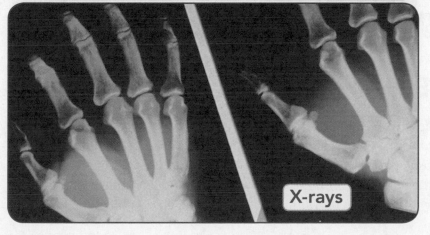

X-rays

Chapter Preview

LESSON 1
- electromagnetic wave
- electromagnetic radiation
- polarized light
- photoelectric effect
- photon

↻ **Identify the Main Idea**
△ **Calculate**

LESSON 2
- electromagnetic spectrum
- radio waves
- microwaves
- radar
- infrared rays
- thermogram
- visible light
- ultraviolet rays
- X-rays
- gamma rays

↻ **Summarize**
△ **Communicate**

LESSON 3
- amplitude modulation
- frequency modulation

↻ **Compare and Contrast**
△ **Interpret Data**

▷ **VOCAB FLASH CARDS** For extra help with vocabulary, visit **Vocab Flash Cards** and type in *Electromagnetic Waves.*

The Nature of Electromagnetic Waves

🔑 **What Makes Up an Electromagnetic Wave?**

🔑 **What Models Explain How Electromagnetic Waves Behave?**

my planet Diary

Posted by: Jordan
Location: Hopkinton, Massachusetts

Life is truly a lot easier with a cell phone. I could contact anybody I would possibly need to, such as my parents or emergency care, if there were an emergency. If I were without a cell phone, who knows what could happen? I like having a cell phone to talk to friends, my parents, and my family. Also, it's easier to have my own phone to use when I want to make a call. Like most people I know, I use my cell phone every day. I can always contact people I need to with a cell phone and it's great to have.

BLOG

Read the following questions. Write your answers below.

1. In what situation might Jordan need to use a cell phone? Who would he call?

_____

_____

_____

2. For what reason would you use a cell phone most?

_____

_____

▶ **PLANET DIARY** Go to **Planet Diary** to learn more about electromagnetic waves.

 Do the Inquiry Warm-Up *How Fast Are Electromagnetic Waves?*

What Makes Up an Electromagnetic Wave?

As you sit at your desk and read this book, you are surrounded by waves you cannot see or hear. There are radio waves, microwaves, infrared rays, visible light, ultraviolet rays, and tiny amounts of X-rays and gamma rays. These waves are all electromagnetic waves.

Vocabulary

- electromagnetic wave
- electromagnetic radiation
- polarized light
- photoelectric effect
- photon

Skills

- Reading: Identify the Main Idea
- Inquiry: Calculate

Characteristics of Electromagnetic Waves

An **electromagnetic wave** is a transverse wave that involves the transfer of electric and magnetic energy. **An electromagnetic wave is made up of vibrating electric and magnetic fields that move through space or some medium at the speed of light.**

An electromagnetic wave can begin with the movement of charged particles, all of which have electric fields around them. As the particles change speed or direction, a vibrating electric field is created, which in turn produces a vibrating magnetic field. The vibrating magnetic field creates a vibrating electric field. The electric and magnetic fields produce each other repeatedly. The result is an electromagnetic wave, shown in **Figure 1.** Note that the two fields vibrate at right angles to one another.

Energy The energy that electromagnetic waves transfer through matter or space is called **electromagnetic radiation.** Electromagnetic waves do not require a medium such as air, so they can transfer energy through a vacuum, or empty space.

FIGURE 1 ·······························

Electromagnetic Wave
An electromagnetic wave travels through space at the speed of light—about 300,000 kilometers per second.

Calculate How long will it take sunlight to travel the 150 million kilometers to Earth? Use a calculator to solve the problem.

_____

_____

_____

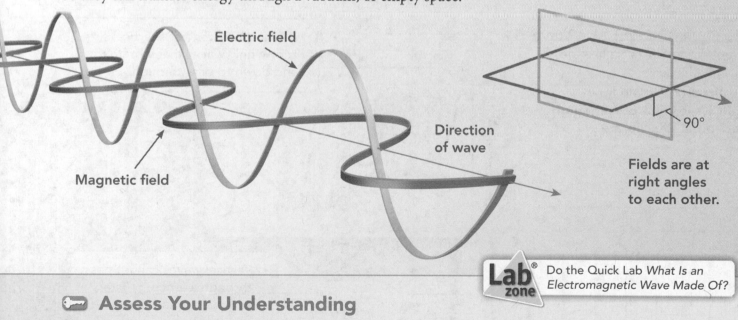

Electric field

Magnetic field

Direction of wave

90°

Fields are at right angles to each other.

Lab zone® Do the Quick Lab *What Is an Electromagnetic Wave Made Of?*

Assess Your Understanding

got it? ·······························

O **I get it!** Now I know that electromagnetic waves are made of _____

_____

O **I need extra help with** _____

Go to **MY SCIENCE** **COACH** *online for help with this subject.*

What Models Explain How Electromagnetic Waves Behave?

Two different models are needed to explain the behavior of electromagnetic waves. A wave model best explains many of the behaviors, but a particle model best explains others. Light is an electromagnetic wave. It has many properties of waves but can also act as though it is a stream of particles.

Wave Model of Light When light passes through a polarizing filter, it has the properties of a wave. An ordinary beam of light consists of waves that vibrate in all directions. A polarizing filter acts as though it has tiny slits aligned in only one direction. The slits can be horizontal or vertical. When light enters a polarizing filter, only some waves can pass through it. The light that passes through is called **polarized light.**

To help you understand the wave model, think of light waves like transverse waves on a rope. They vibrate in all directions. If you shake a rope through a fence with vertical slits, only waves that vibrate up and down will pass through, as shown in **Figure 2.** The other waves are blocked. A polarizing filter acts like the slits in a fence. It allows only waves that vibrate in one direction to pass through it.

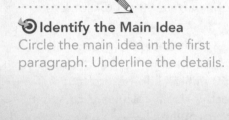

Identify the Main Idea
Circle the main idea in the first paragraph. Underline the details.

FIGURE 2 ·······················
▶ VIRTUAL LAB **Light as a Wave**
A polarizing filter acts like the slits in a fence.

✎ **Predict** Explain how light waves that pass through horizontal slits vibrate.

_____

_____

_____

_____

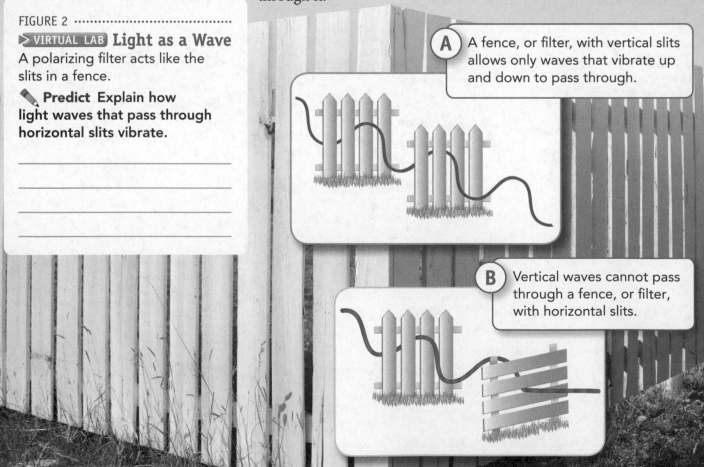

A A fence, or filter, with vertical slits allows only waves that vibrate up and down to pass through.

B Vertical waves cannot pass through a fence, or filter, with horizontal slits.

apply it!

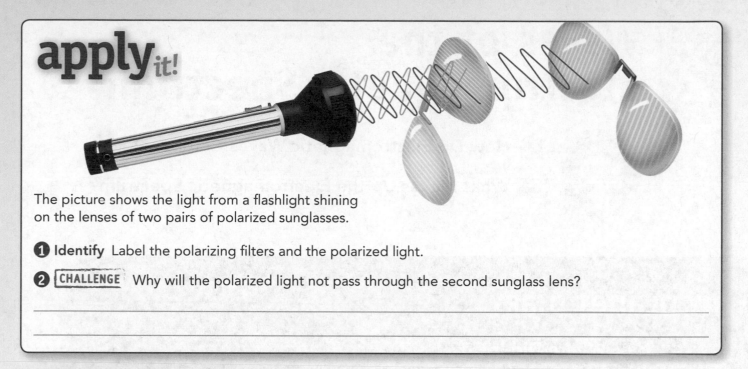

The picture shows the light from a flashlight shining on the lenses of two pairs of polarized sunglasses.

1 **Identify** Label the polarizing filters and the polarized light.

2 **CHALLENGE** Why will the polarized light not pass through the second sunglass lens?

_____

_____

Particle Model of Light
Sometimes light behaves like a stream of particles. For example, when a beam of high frequency light shines on some metals, it causes tiny particles to move. These particles are called electrons. Sometimes light can even cause an electron to move so much that it is knocked out of the metal, as shown in **Figure 3.** This is called the **photoelectric effect.** This effect can be explained by thinking of light as a stream of tiny packets, or particles, of energy. Each packet of light energy is called a **photon.** For the effect to occur, each photon must contain enough energy to knock an electron free from the metal.

FIGURE 3 ···
The Photoelectric Effect
Photons hitting a metal surface knock out electrons.

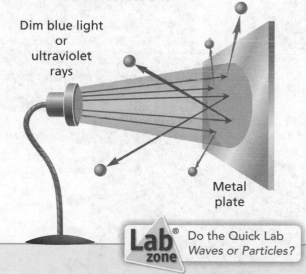

Dim blue light or ultraviolet rays

Metal plate

Lab ® **zone** Do the Quick Lab
Waves or Particles?

🔑 Assess Your Understanding

1a. Define A _____ is a tiny packet of energy.

b. Describe What does a polarizing filter do?

_____

_____

_____

got it?

○ **I get it!** Now I know that the models that explain how electromagnetic waves behave are _____

_____

○ **I need extra help with** _____

_Go to_ **my science** 🔵 **coach** _online for help with this subject._

Waves of the Electromagnetic Spectrum

UNLOCK THE BIG Q

🔑 **How Do Electromagnetic Waves Compare?**

🔑 **What Makes Up the Electromagnetic Spectrum?**

my planet DiaRY

DISCOVERY

Hey, Where Did It Go?

What would you do if you had an invisibility cloak? This idea might not be as far-fetched as it sounds. Scientists have actually been working on creating a way to make objects invisible! Researchers have created a device that can change the direction of microwaves, so that they flow around a test object. This rerouting causes the object to look invisible at microwave frequencies. Unfortunately, people cannot see microwaves, which means the object isn't invisible to us. But, who knows, maybe one day you'll be able to put on one of these "cloaks" and move around completely unseen!

Answer the question below.

If a device like this is developed for visible light, how do you think a scientist who studies animals in nature might use it?

_____

_____

_____

_____

_____

▶ PLANET DIARY Go to **Planet Diary** to learn more about the electromagnetic spectrum.

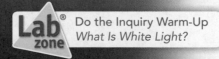

Lab® zone Do the Inquiry Warm-Up _What Is White Light?_

Vocabulary
- electromagnetic spectrum • radio waves • microwaves
- radar • infrared rays • thermogram • visible light
- ultraviolet rays • X-rays • gamma rays

Skills
- Reading: Summarize
- Inquiry: Communicate

How Do Electromagnetic Waves Compare?

Can you imagine trying to take a photo with a radio or heating your food with X-rays? Light, radio waves, and X-rays are all electromagnetic waves. But each has properties that make it more useful for some purposes than others. **All electromagnetic waves travel at the same speed in a vacuum, but they have different wavelengths and different frequencies.** A vacuum is a space that contains no air or other gas.

Visible light is the only range of wavelengths your eyes can see. Your radio detects radio waves, which have much longer wavelengths than visible light. X-rays, on the other hand, have much shorter wavelengths than visible light.

For waves in any medium, as the wavelength decreases, the frequency increases. Waves with the longest wavelengths have the lowest frequencies. Waves with the shortest wavelengths have the highest frequencies. The higher the frequency of a wave, the higher its energy.

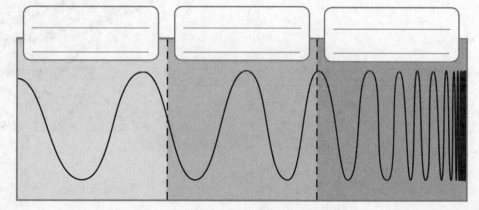

FIGURE 1 ···

Comparing Electromagnetic Waves

Different types of electromagnetic waves have different wavelengths.

✏️ **Complete these tasks.**

1. **Label** Write the names *visible light*, *radio waves*, and *X-rays* in the correct boxes on the diagram.

2. **Draw Conclusions** Which wave has the highest energy? Explain.

_____
_____
_____
_____
_____

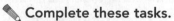
Lab zone Do the Quick Lab *Differences Between Waves.*

🔑 Assess Your Understanding

got it? ···

○ **I get it!** Now I know that electromagnetic waves have different _____
_____ but the same _____

○ **I need extra help with** _____

Go to my science ⓢ coach *online for help with this subject.*

What Makes Up the Electromagnetic Spectrum?

There are many different types of electromagnetic waves. The complete range of electromagnetic waves placed in order of increasing frequency is called the **electromagnetic spectrum.** 🔑 **The electromagnetic spectrum is made up of radio waves, microwaves, infrared rays, visible light, ultraviolet rays, X-rays, and gamma rays.** The full spectrum is shown in **Figure 2.**

Radio Waves Electromagnetic waves with the longest wavelengths and the lowest frequencies are **radio waves.** Radio waves are used in broadcasting to carry signals for radio programs. A broadcast station sends out radio waves at certain frequencies. Your radio picks up the radio waves and converts them into an electrical signal. The electrical signal is then converted into sound.

FIGURE 2 ···

The Electromagnetic Spectrum

The electromagnetic spectrum can be broken up into different categories.

✎ **Interpret Diagrams** Use the word bank to fill in the boxes in the diagram. Do microwaves or ultraviolet waves have longer wavelengths? Which have higher frequencies?

_____

_____

_____

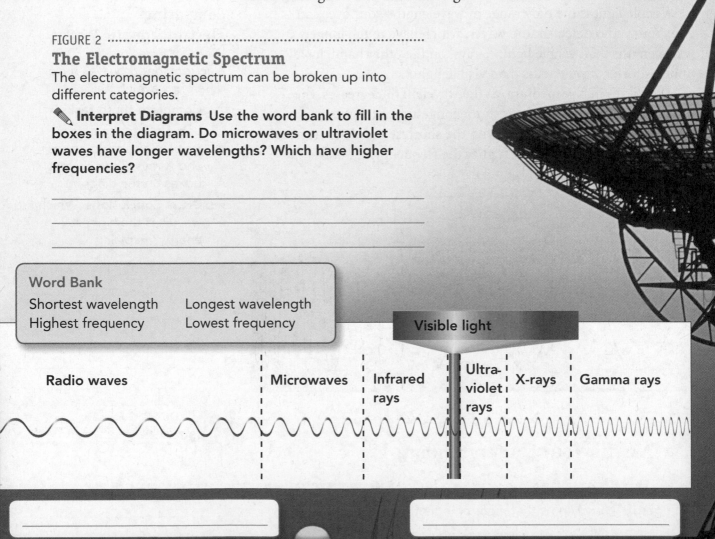

Word Bank

Shortest wavelength   Longest wavelength
Highest frequency   Lowest frequency

Visible light

Radio waves   Microwaves   Infrared rays   Ultra-violet rays   X-rays   Gamma rays

Microwaves

Microwaves have shorter wavelengths and higher frequencies than radio waves do. When you think about microwaves, you probably think of microwave ovens that cook and heat food. But microwaves have many other uses, including cellular phone communication and radar.

Radar stands for **ra**dio **d**etection **an**d **r**anging. **Radar** is a system that uses reflected microwaves to detect objects and measure their distance and speed. To measure distance, a radar device sends out microwaves that reflect off an object. The time it takes for the reflected waves to return is used to calculate the object's distance. To measure speed, a radar device uses the Doppler effect. For example, suppose a police radar gun sends out microwaves that reflect off a car. Because the car is moving, the frequency of the reflected waves is different from the frequency of the original waves. The difference in frequency is used to calculate the car's speed.

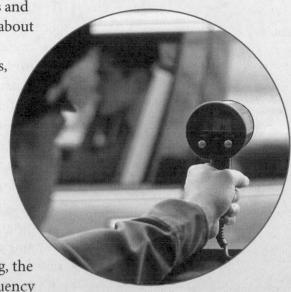

apply it!

Radio stations are broadcast in two different frequency ranges. The ranges are the kilohertz range (kHz) for AM stations and the megahertz range (MHz) for FM stations. The prefix *kilo-* means "thousand"; *mega-* means "million."

1 Interpret Data What is the frequency range of the AM band on the radio? Of the FM band?

_____

_____

2 Interpret Photos Approximately what frequencies are being tuned in on each band?

_____

_____

3 CHALLENGE The units kHz and MHz stand for kilohertz and megahertz, respectively. If 1 MHz = 1000 kHz, which waves (AM or FM) have longer wavelengths? Explain.

_____

_____

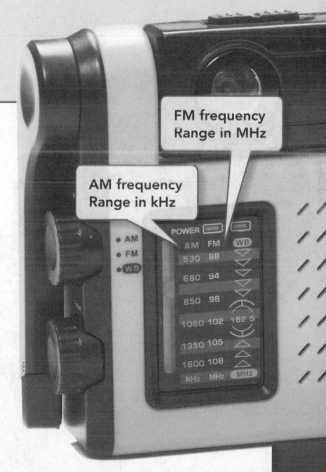

FM frequency Range in MHz

AM frequency Range in kHz

Vocabulary Greek Word **Origins** The prefix *thermo-* comes from the Greek word *thermos* which means "warm or hot." How does this meaning relate to the definition of *thermogram*?

_____

_____

_____

_____

_____

Infrared Rays If you turn on an electric stove's burner, you can feel it warm up before the heating element starts to glow. The invisible heat you feel is infrared radiation, or infrared rays. **Infrared rays** are electromagnetic waves with wavelengths shorter than those of microwaves. They have higher frequencies and therefore more energy than microwaves. Because you can feel the energy of infrared rays as heat, these rays are often called heat rays. Heat lamps have bulbs that give off mainly infrared rays. They are used to keep things warm, such as food in a cafeteria or young animals in an incubator.

Most objects give off some infrared rays. Warmer objects give off infrared rays with more energy and higher frequencies than cooler objects. An infrared camera uses infrared rays instead of visible light to take pictures called thermograms. A **thermogram** is an image that shows regions of different temperatures in different colors, as shown in **Figure 3**.

FIGURE 3 ·······································

The Uses of Infrared Rays
Infrared rays are used in devices such as heat lamps and TV remote controls.

✎ **Complete these tasks.**

1. **Interpret Diagrams** List the labeled areas on the thermogram from hottest to coolest.

_____

Heat lamp

2. **Identify** Where do you think this heat lamp is being used?

_____

_____

_____

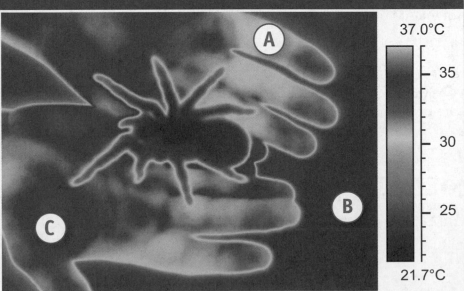

Thermogram

37.0°C

35

30

25

21.7°C

Visible light waves with the longest wavelengths appear red in color.

The shortest wavelengths of visible light appear violet in color.

Sequence What are the colors of the visible spectrum in order, starting with red?

_____

_____

_____

Interpret Photos Which color has the highest frequency?

_____

_____

FIGURE 4 ···

The Visible Spectrum

Refraction of white light from the sun by raindrops separates the light into the colors of the visible spectrum.

 **Answer the questions in the boxes to the left and below.**

Communicate Talk with a partner. Describe other times when you have seen the visible spectrum.

_____

_____

_____

_____

_____

_____

_____

Visible Light

Electromagnetic waves that you can see are called **visible light.** They make up only a small part of the electromagnetic spectrum. Visible light waves have shorter wavelengths and higher frequencies than infrared rays.

Visible light that appears white is actually a mixture of many colors. Recall that light waves bend, or refract, when they enter a new medium. So, when white light passes through rain drops, a rainbow can result, like the one in **Figure 4**.

Ultraviolet Rays

Electromagnetic waves with wavelengths just shorter than those of visible light are called **ultraviolet rays.** Ultraviolet rays have higher frequencies than visible light, so they carry more energy. The energy of ultraviolet rays can damage or kill living cells. For example, too much exposure to ultraviolet rays can burn your skin and over time may cause skin cancer. However, small doses of ultraviolet rays are useful. They cause skin cells to produce vitamin D, which is needed for healthy bones and teeth.

did you know?

The Environmental Protection Agency of the United States tracks ultraviolet light levels in Texas and throughout the country. The agency's UV index rates ultraviolet exposure on a scale of 1 to 11+. High ratings result in UV exposure warnings. These warnings let people know how long they can be out in the sun safely without sunblock.

77

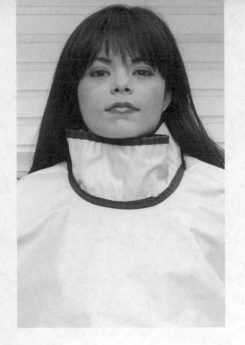

FIGURE 5 ·····································

Lead Apron

X-rays are often used to look at bones and teeth.

✎ **Explain** Why does a dentist cover you with a lead apron to take X-rays of your teeth?

_____

_____

_____

_____

·· ✎ ··

🔄 **Summarize** In your own words, write a summary of the section about gamma rays.

X-rays Electromagnetic waves with wavelengths just shorter than those of ultraviolet rays are **X-rays.** Their frequencies are just a little higher than ultraviolet rays. Because of their high frequencies, X-rays carry more energy than ultraviolet rays and can penetrate most matter. Dense matter, such as bone or lead, absorbs X-rays so they do not pass through. Therefore, X-rays are used to make images of bones and teeth. However, too much exposure to X-rays can cause cancer. See **Figure 5.**

X-rays can also be used in industry and engineering. Engineers can use an X-ray image of a steel or concrete structure to find cracks. Dark areas on the X-ray film show the cracks.

Gamma Rays Electromagnetic waves with the shortest wavelengths and highest frequencies are **gamma rays.** Since they have the greatest amount of energy, gamma rays are the most penetrating of electromagnetic waves. Because of their penetrating ability, these rays are used to examine the body's internal structures. A patient can be injected with a fluid that emits gamma rays. Then, a gamma-ray detector can form an image of the inside of the body.

Some radioactive substances and certain nuclear reactions produce gamma rays. Some objects in space emit bursts of gamma rays. However, these rays are blocked by Earth's atmosphere. Astronomers think that explosions of distant stars produce these gamma rays.

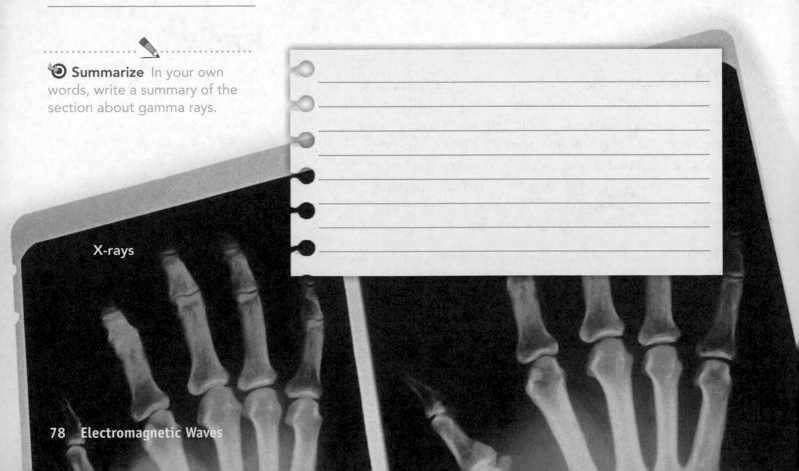

X-rays

Surfing the Spectrum

What kinds of waves make up the electromagnetic spectrum?

FIGURE 6 ···

> **INTERACTIVE ART** The electromagnetic spectrum includes many kinds of waves.

✏ **Complete the activities.**

1. **Identify** Label each kind of wave on the electromagnetic spectrum.

2. **Classify** Circle the name of the highest energy waves.

3. **Apply Concepts** On the notebook page, describe the uses of two kinds of waves.

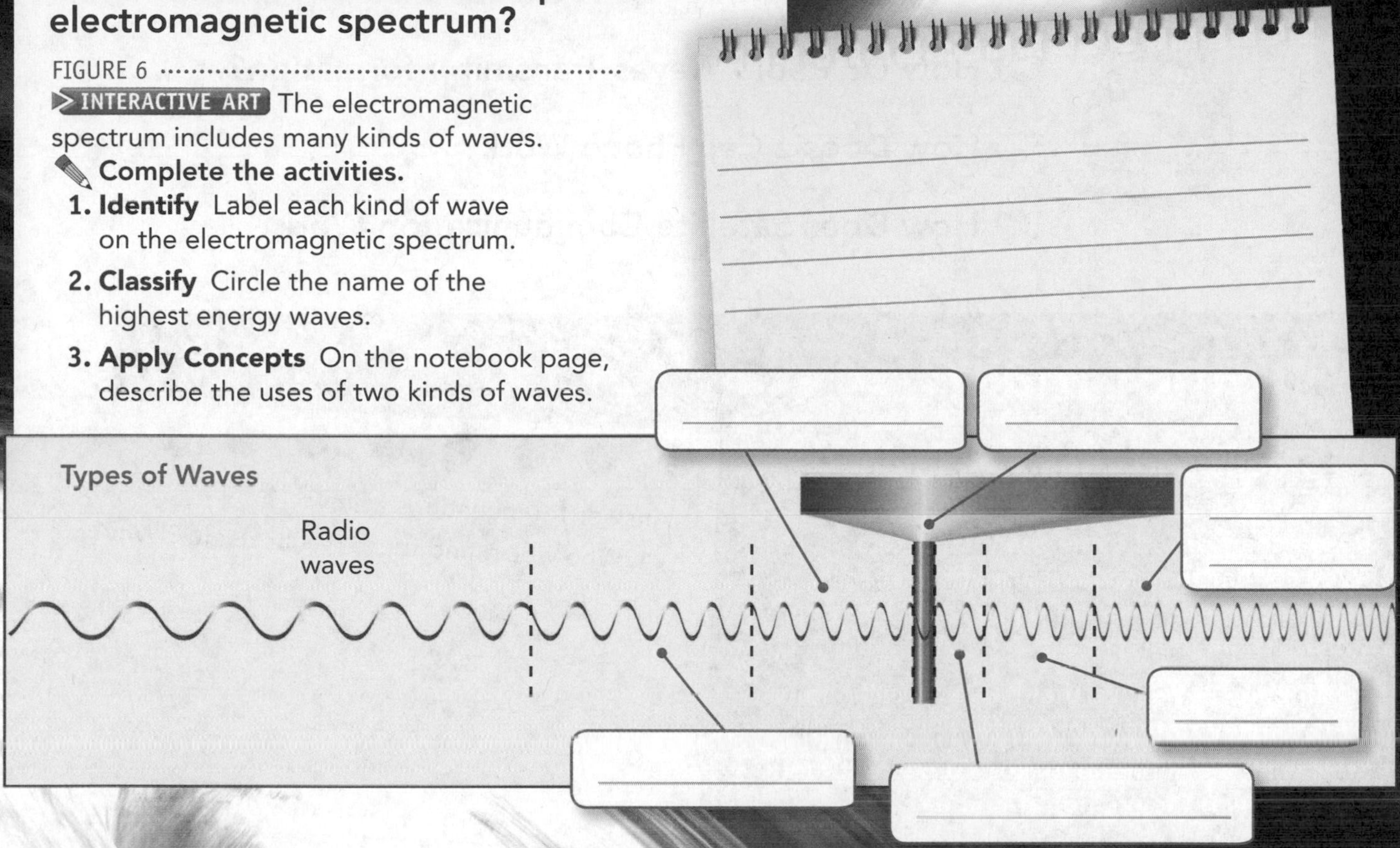

Types of Waves

Radio waves

Lab zone® Do the Quick Lab *Parts of the Electromagnetic Spectrum.*

🔑 Assess Your Understanding

1a. Explain How do ultraviolet rays help your bones and teeth?

_____

_____

_____

_____

b. ANSWER THE BIG ? What kinds of waves make up the electromagnetic spectrum?

_____

_____

_____

_____

_____

got it? ···

○ **I get it!** Now I know the electromagnetic spectrum is made up of _____

_____

○ **I need extra help with** _____

Go to **MY SCIENCE** Ⓢ **COACH** online for help with this subject.

Wireless Communication

UNLOCK
THE BIG

🔑 **How Do Radio Waves Transmit Information?**

🔑 **How Does a Cell Phone Work?**

🔑 **How Does Satellite Communication Work?**

my PLaneT DiaRY

Teens and Their Cell Phones

How do teens feel about cell phones? Researchers asked some teens to take a survey so that they could learn about teens' cell-phone usage. How do these results compare with your own ideas?

- 45 percent believe that having a cell phone is the key to their social life.

- Having a cell phone makes 78 percent feel safe when they're not at home.

- When asked to select additional features for a basic cell phone, 71 percent chose a music player.

- More than half use cell phones to check e-mail.

- Nearly half said they could send text messages while blindfolded!

FUN FACTS

Answer the questions below.

1. Who would find these results useful? Why?

_____

_____

_____

_____

_____

2. What do you think is the most important use of a cell phone?

_____

_____

▷ PLANET DIARY Go to **Planet Diary** to learn more about wireless communication.

Lab zone® Do the Inquiry Warm-Up *How Can Waves Change?*

Vocabulary
- amplitude modulation
- frequency modulation

Skills
- ↻ Reading: Compare and Contrast
- △ Inquiry: Interpret Data

How Do Radio Waves Transmit Information?

You are in the car on a long road trip and switch on the radio to listen to some music. In an instant, your favorite song is coming through the car's speakers. How do radio broadcasts reach you?

Broadcasting Radio waves carry, or transmit, signals for radio programs. Charged particles vibrating inside transmission antennas produce radio waves. Transmission antennas send out, or broadcast, radio waves in many directions. 🔑 **Radio waves carry information from the antenna of a broadcasting station to the receiving antenna of your radio.** Look at **Figure 1.**

FIGURE 1 ·····································

How a Radio Works
Radios tune in radio wave signals broadcast by antennas located at radio stations.

✏️ **Sequence** In the circles, number the steps to show the correct order of events that results in hearing a broadcast.

Radio waves strike your radio's antenna and are picked up.

The electronic signal comes out of your radio as sound.

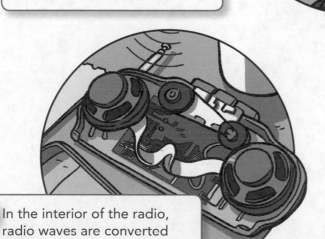

In the interior of the radio, radio waves are converted into an electronic signal.

At the radio station, electronics convert music into radio waves that are then broadcast by a large antenna.

FIGURE 2 ⋯⋯⋯⋯⋯⋯⋯⋯⋯⋯⋯⋯⋯

> INTERACTIVE ART **Radio Waves**
Radio stations transmit signals
by changing a radio wave's
amplitude or frequency.

✎ **Interpret Diagrams** Under
each type of wave, write the
wave property that is constant.

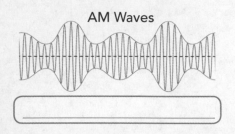

AM Waves

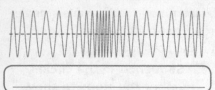

FM Waves

✎ **Compare and Contrast**
Complete the Venn diagram
to compare AM and FM
radio waves.

Broadcasting Signals Radio stations broadcast signals in
two frequency bands. These bands are amplitude modulation (AM)
and frequency modulation (FM).

Amplitude Modulation A method of broadcasting signals by
changing the amplitude of a wave is called **amplitude modulation**.
AM signals travel as changes, or modulations, in the amplitude of
the wave. The frequency of an AM wave is constant.

AM radio waves have relatively long wavelengths and low
frequencies and energy. They are easily reflected back to Earth's
surface by Earth's ionosphere, a region of charged particles high
in the atmosphere. Therefore, AM radio stations can be broadcast
over long distances.

Frequency Modulation **Frequency modulation** is a method
of broadcasting signals by changing the frequency of a wave.
FM signals travel as changes in the frequency of the wave. The
amplitude of an FM wave is constant.

FM waves have higher frequencies and more energy than
AM waves. FM waves pass through the ionosphere instead of being
reflected back to Earth. Therefore, they do not travel as far on
Earth's surface as AM waves. However, FM waves usually produce
better sound quality than AM waves. **Figure 2** shows FM waves and
AM waves.

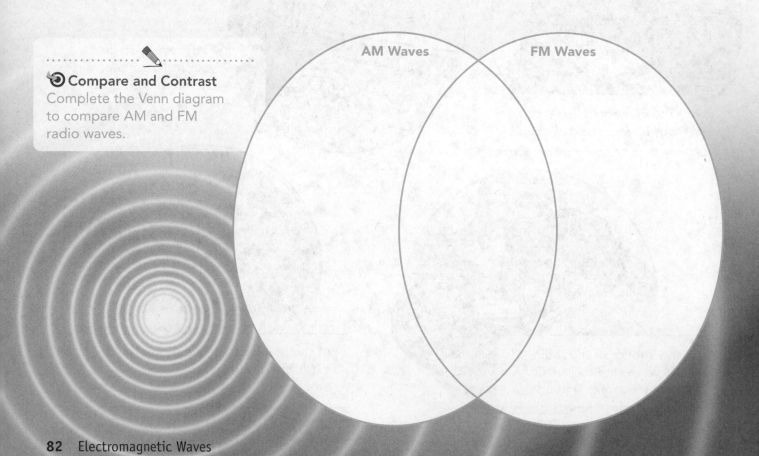

AM Waves   FM Waves

do the math! Analyzing Data

The table shows the frequencies assigned by the Federal Communications Commission (FCC) for various radio channels.

1 Interpret Data Which broadcast uses the highest-frequency range? Which uses the lowest-frequency range?

_____

_____

_____

_____

_____

Broadcast Frequencies		
Type of Broadcast	Frequency Range	Converted Frequency Range
AM radio	535 kHz to 1,605 kHz	
Amateur radio	1,800 kHz to 1,900 kHz	
FM radio	88 MHz to 108 MHz	

2 CHALLENGE Convert each given frequency range into units of hertz. (*Hint:* 1 kHz = 1000 Hz, and 1 MHz = 1,000,000 Hz.) Write your answers in the table.

The Radio Spectrum
In addition to AM and FM broadcasts, radio waves are used for many types of communication. The FCC assigns different radio frequencies for different uses. Radio stations use one part of the radio spectrum. Taxi and police radios are assigned separate sets of frequencies. Amateur radio frequencies are assigned for people who operate radios as a hobby. Because the signals all have different assigned frequencies, they travel without interfering.

Lab zone Do the Lab Investigation *Build a Crystal Radio.*

🔑 Assess Your Understanding

1a. Identify What wave property is changed when AM radio signals are broadcast?

_____

b. Apply Concepts Longer wavelengths bend more easily around obstacles such as mountains. In a hilly countryside, will you be more likely to hear an AM or FM station?

_____

_____

got it?

○ **I get it!** Now I know that radio waves _____

_____

_____

○ **I need extra help with** _____

Go to **MY SCIENCE ⑤ COACH** online for help with this subject.

How Does a Cell Phone Work?

Cellular telephones, or cell phones, are an important part of your daily life. However, they only work if they are in a cellular system. The cellular system works by dividing regions into many small cells, or geographical areas, as shown in **Figure 3**. Each cell has one or more towers that relay signals to a central hub.

Cell phones transmit and receive signals using high-frequency microwaves. Though the process needed to complete a cell phone call looks complicated, the entire process happens so quickly it seems to be instantaneous. In addition to making phone calls, cell phones have many different uses. They can be used to send text messages, browse the Internet, and take photos.

A

1 When you place a cell-phone call, the phone sends out microwaves, which are tagged with a number unique to your phone.

2 A tower picks up the microwaves and transfers the signal to a hub.

3 The hub channels and transmits the signal to a receiver. The receiver may be another tower or another hub, depending on the distance between the two phones.

4 The tower or hub transmits the signal to the receiving cell phone.

FIGURE 3

> ART IN MOTION **Using a Cell Phone**

The quality of your cell-phone calls depends on the terrain and how close your phone is to a cell-phone tower or a central hub.

✎ **Apply Concepts** Suppose you make a call from location B to a friend at location C. Draw the path the signal could travel to complete the call. Explain what would likely happen if you made a cell call from location A.

_____

_____

_____

5 The receiving phone rings when it picks up the signal.

Lab® zone Do the Quick Lab *How Cell Phones Work.*

🔑 **Assess Your Understanding**

2a. Infer What happens if your cell phone is far away from a tower?

_____

_____

_____

b. Draw Conclusions Your cell phone sends out a signal at a specific frequency. What will happen if a cell phone next to you also uses this frequency?

_____

_____

_____

got it? ....

○ **I get it!** Now I know that cell phones work by _____

_____

_____

○ I need extra help with _____

Go to my science ⒮ coach *online for help with this subject.*

85

How Does Satellite Communication Work?

Satellites orbiting Earth send information around the world. Communications satellites work like the receivers and transmitters of a cellular phone system. ⟳ **Communications satellites receive radio, television, and telephone signals and relay the signals to receivers on Earth.** Because a satellite can "see" only part of Earth at any time, more than one satellite is needed for any purpose.

Satellite Phone Systems Several companies offer satellite phone systems. Radio waves from one phone are sent up to a communications satellite. The satellite transmits the waves back to the receiving phone on Earth. With this kind of phone, you can call anywhere in the world, but it costs more than using a cell phone.

Satellite Television Systems Television networks and cable companies use communications satellites. Television signals are sent up to satellites. The satellites then relay the signals to places around the world. Television signals from satellites are often scrambled. Customers of satellite companies need a satellite dish antenna like the one shown in **Figure 4** to pick up the signals and a decoding box to unscramble the signals.

✎ **Compare and Contrast**
In the paragraphs to the right, underline the sentences that compare satellite communication with another form of electronic communication.

FIGURE 4 ·······································
Satellite Dishes
Dish-shaped antennas receive signals for television programs from satellites.

✎ **Infer** Satellite dishes point to a fixed location in the sky. What does this tell you about the position of the satellite?

_____

_____

_____

_____

Global Positioning System

The Global Positioning System (GPS) is a system of navigation originally designed for the military. GPS uses a network of 24 satellites that broadcast radio signals to Earth. These signals carry information that tells you your exact location on Earth's surface, or even in the air. Anybody with a GPS receiver can pick up these signals. GPS receivers can be found in cars, airplanes, boats, and even cell phones.

Signals from four out of 24 GPS satellites are used to determine your position. The signals from three satellites tell you where you are on Earth's surface. The signal from the fourth satellite tells you how far above Earth's surface you are.

GPS unit in car

GPS satellite

FIGURE 5 ···

> ART IN MOTION **Uses of Satellites**

Modern communication uses satellites in different ways.

✎ **Summarize** Complete the table by summarizing how satellites are used in each type of communication.

System	Summary
Global Positioning System	
Satellite Phone System	
Television Satellites	

Lab zone | Do the Quick Lab *How Does GPS Work?*

🔑 Assess Your Understanding

got it? ···

○ **I get it!** Now I know that satellites work by _____

_____

○ **I need extra help with** _____

Go to MY SCIENCE ⓢ COACH *online for help with this subject.*

Study Guide

The electromagnetic spectrum is made up of radio waves, _____,
_____, visible light, _____, _____, and gamma rays.

LESSON 1 The Nature of Electromagnetic Waves

🔑 An electromagnetic wave is made up of vibrating electric
and magnetic fields that move through space or some medium
at the speed of light.

🔑 Two different models are needed to explain the behavior
of electromagnetic waves. A wave model best explains many of
the behaviors, but a particle model best explains others.

Vocabulary
- electromagnetic wave • electromagnetic radiation
- polarized light • photoelectric effect • photon

LESSON 2 Waves of the Electromagnetic Spectrum

🔑 All electromagnetic waves travel at the same speed
in a vacuum, but they have different wavelengths and different
frequencies.

🔑 The electromagnetic spectrum is made up of radio waves,
microwaves, infrared rays, visible light, ultraviolet rays, X-rays,
and gamma rays.

Vocabulary
- electromagnetic spectrum • radio waves • microwaves • radar
- infrared rays • thermogram • visible light • ultraviolet rays
- X-rays • gamma rays

LESSON 3 Wireless Communication

🔑 Radio waves carry information from the antenna of a
broadcasting station to the receiving antenna of your radio.

🔑 Cell phones transmit and receive signals using
high-frequency microwaves.

🔑 Communications satellites receive radio, television,
and telephone signals and relay the signals to receivers
on Earth.

Vocabulary
- amplitude modulation • frequency modulation

Review and Assessment

LESSON 1 The Nature of Electromagnetic Waves

1. An electromagnetic wave consists of
   a. AM and FM waves.
   b. electrons and protons.
   c. electric and magnetic fields.
   d. particles of a medium.

2. The _____ model of light describes the behavior of light when it acts as a stream of photons.

3. **Compare and Contrast** Explain how polarized light is different from non-polarized light.

   _____
   _____
   _____
   _____
   _____

4. **Observe** How do you know that electromagnetic waves can travel through a vacuum?

   _____
   _____
   _____
   _____

5. **Write About It** Suppose you go shopping for sunglasses with a friend. He likes a pair of sunglasses labeled *polarized lenses.* Using what you learned in this lesson, explain to him how polarizing sunglasses work.

LESSON 2 Waves of the Electromagnetic Spectrum

6. The electromagnetic waves with the longest wavelengths and lowest frequencies are
   a. radio waves.   b. infrared rays.
   c. X-rays.   d. gamma rays.

7. _____ is the only type of electromagnetic wave that you can see.

Use the graph below to answer Questions 8 and 9.

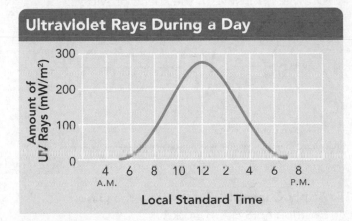

8. **Interpret Graphs** What is the amount of ultraviolet rays at 8 P.M.?

   _____

9. **Infer** What is the cause of the peak in the graph line at 12 P.M.?

   _____
   _____

10. **Classify** Night vision goggles allow you to see warm objects in a dark environment. Which type of electromagnetic wave do they detect?

    _____
    _____

LESSON 3 Wireless Communication

11. What is the ionosphere?

    a. a type of AM radio wave

    b. a region of charged particles
       in Earth's atmosphere

    c. the region of a cell-phone network

    d. a type of FM radio wave

12. Cell phones transmit and receive signals using

_____

13. Make Models An AM wave is shown below.
Draw an FM wave in the space provided.

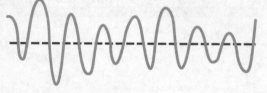

AM wave

FM wave

14. Apply Concepts Explain how the Global
Positioning System works.

_____

_____

_____

_____

15. Write About It You are going on a car trip with
your family across the United States. To your
brother's surprise, the AM radio station that
your family is listening to is coming from a city
1,000 kilometers away. Explain to him how this
is possible. Be sure to describe how the ionosphere affects AM radio transmissions.

 **What kinds of waves make
up the electromagnetic
spectrum?**

16. Many everyday technologies with which you
come in contact use electromagnetic waves.
Choose four objects from the picture below
and describe the kinds of electromagnetic
waves that they use. List your answer in
order of increasing energy of the waves
each object uses.

_____

_____

_____

_____

_____

_____

_____

_____

Standardized Test Prep

Multiple Choice

Circle the letter of the best answer.

1. What would you add to the picture below so that light does not hit the final screen?

   A another light bulb
   B a filter with horizontal slits
   C a filter with vertical slits
   D none of the above

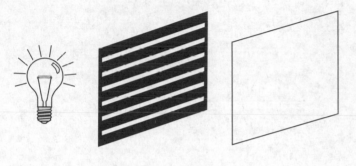

2. Ultraviolet rays from the sun are able to reach Earth's surface because

   A they require air to travel through.
   B they have less energy than infrared rays.
   C they have lower frequency than visible light.
   D they can travel through empty space.

3. Which of the following groups of electromagnetic waves is listed correctly in order of increasing energy?

   A X-rays, visible light, radio waves
   B radio waves, visible light, X-rays
   C infrared rays, visible light, radio waves
   D visible light, gamma rays, X-rays

4. Radar is a system that

   A detects objects and measures their speed.
   B kills bacteria.
   C carries AM signals.
   D searches for hidden objects.

5. AM radio waves are able to travel farther than FM radio waves because

   A AM waves produce better sound quality.
   B AM waves are reflected by Earth's ionosphere.
   C AM waves are faster than FM waves.
   D AM waves have constant amplitude.

Constructed Response

Use your knowledge of science to help you answer Question 6. Write your answer on a separate sheet of paper.

6. Explain how the visible spectrum is formed as a rainbow appears after it rains. In your answer, explain what white light is composed of.

Channel Surfin'
on an
Infrared WAVE

You have access to an entire world of entertainment and information at the push of a button, and you don't have to leave your chair. When you push the buttons on your remote control, it uses infrared light (an invisible part of the electromagnetic spectrum) to send signals to an electronic device.

When you press a button on a TV remote control, it sends out pulses of infrared light. These pulses contain a binary code. A binary code consists of a combination of the numbers 1 and 0. Each command on the remote control has a different binary code. For example, on one type of remote the command for "channel up" is 001 0000. The command for "channel down" is 001 0001. The TV's microprocessor, or the brain of the TV, interprets and carries out the correct command.

So why doesn't that remote control turn on the CD player or the microwave? To avoid interference from other infrared light sources, such as the sun and fluorescent light bulbs, each remote control uses a specific wavelength for its signals. As a result, other electronic devices won't respond to the infrared signals from the TV remote control.

Research It Research how a remote control can use both infrared light and radio frequencies. Design a device that uses both types of waves and explain how the device works and how it can be used.

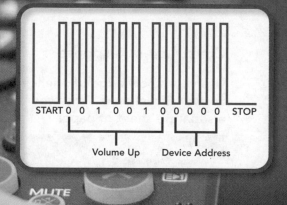

START 0 0 1 0 0 1 0 0 0 0 0 STOP

Volume Up   Device Address

Museum of Science.

Healing With MAGNETISM?

Magnetism is a powerful force with many uses. One claim is that it can relieve pain. The idea is that the magnetic field of a copper bracelet ionizes blood traveling through the wearer's wrist. This is supposed to change the electronic charge in the molecules of the blood. Supporters claim that the newly ionized blood improves circulation and oxygen flow. But what is really going on?

Doctors have done studies to test the claims made about these bracelets. A placebo is a control substance in experiments—something that looks like the material being tested, but doesn't do anything to the subject. In these studies, some patients wore ionic bracelets and others wore placebo bracelets, which looked the same but were not ionic. Doctors found no statistical difference in the pain relief from wearing an ionic bracelet versus a placebo bracelet. That means the bracelets don't work, but people experience pain relief because they believe the bracelets work. It's mind over matter!

Test It Find several sources presenting claims about magnetic bracelets. Write a letter to a friend who is considering buying one of these bracelets. Evaluate the claims made in the ads, and help your friend make an informed decision.

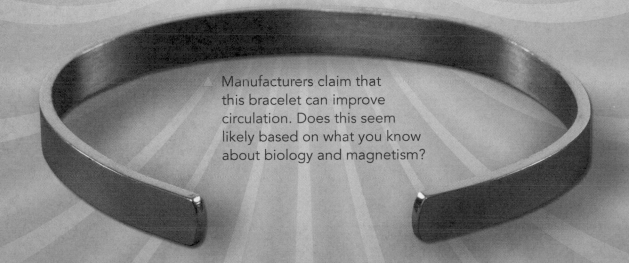

Manufacturers claim that this bracelet can improve circulation. Does this seem likely based on what you know about biology and magnetism?

WHY CAN YOU SEE A CITY IN THIS SCULPTURE?

How does light interact with matter?

Cloud Gate, a 110-ton sculpture in Chicago, Illinois, is made of highly polished stainless steel. The buildings that you see in the sculpture are a reflection of the city of Chicago.

Predict If you were standing directly in front of this sculpture, what would you see? Explain your answer.

_____

_____

_____

_____

_____

_____

> UNTAMED SCIENCE Watch the **Untamed Science** video to learn more about light.

Light

4 Getting Started

Check Your Understanding

1. **Background** Read the paragraph below and then answer the question.

Jamal wakes up early to write a term paper. As the sun rises, it **transmits** sunlight through the window. The light **reflects** off of his computer screen, making it difficult for him to read the words he types. He pulls down the window shade knowing it will **absorb** some of the light.

> To **transmit** is to pass something from one place to another.
>
> To **reflect** is to throw something back.
>
> To **absorb** is to take something in or soak it up.

- Why does the window create a problem for Jamal?

_____

_____

> **MY READING WEB** If you had trouble completing the question above, visit **My Reading Web** and type in *Light.*

Vocabulary Skill

Use Prefixes A prefix is a word part that is added at the beginning of a root or base word to change its meaning. Knowing the meaning of prefixes will help you figure out new words.

Prefix	Meaning	Example
micro-	small, tiny	microscope
tele-	distant, operating at a distance	telescope
con-	together with, jointly	concave mirror, convex mirror
trans-	through	translucent

2. **Quick Check** Choose the word from the table that best completes the sentence.

You need a _____ to view the planets in any detail.

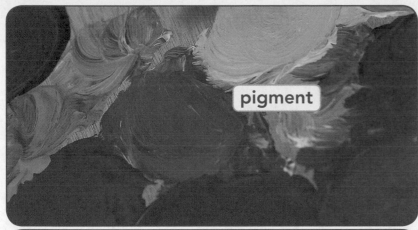

pigment

plane mirror

mirage

convex lens

Chapter Preview

LESSON 1

- transparent - translucent
- opaque - primary color
- secondary color
- complementary color - pigment

⟳ Identify the Main Idea

△ Predict

LESSON 2

- ray - regular reflection - image
- diffuse reflection - plane mirror
- virtual image - concave mirror
- optical axis - focal point
- real image - convex mirror

⟳ Compare and Contrast

△ Classify

LESSON 3

- index of refraction - mirage
- lens - concave lens
- convex lens

⟳ Ask Questions

△ Interpret Data

LESSON 4

- cornea - pupil - iris - retina
- rods - cones - optic nerve
- nearsighted - farsighted

⟳ Sequence

△ Observe

LESSON 5

- camera - telescope
- refracting telescope - objective
- eyepiece - reflecting telescope
- microscope

⟳ Relate Text and Visuals

△ Infer

▷ VOCAB FLASH CARDS For extra help with vocabulary, visit **Vocab Flash Cards** and type in *Light*.

Light and Color

UNLOCK THE BIG **?**

🔑 **What Determines Color?**

🔑 **How Do Colors Combine?**

my PLANET DiaRY

FUN FACTS

Why Is the Sky Blue?

Why does the sky look blue on a clear, sunny day? The answer has to do with the nature of light.

The sun gives off white light. White light is made up of many colors. The different colors of light have different wavelengths. Red light has a longer wavelength than blue light. As the sun's light passes through our atmosphere, gas molecules in the air scatter the sunlight. The blue wavelengths get scattered the most, so the sky appears blue!

Communicate Discuss this question with a classmate. Then write your answer below.

The water droplets in clouds scatter all of the wavelengths of visible light equally. How does this explain why clouds are white?

_____

_____

_____

_____

▶ PLANET DIARY Go to **Planet Diary** to learn more about color.

 Do the Inquiry Warm-Up *How Do Colors Mix?*

What Determines Color?

Why is the grass green or a daffodil yellow? To understand why objects have different colors, you need to know how light can interact with an object. When light strikes an object, the light can be reflected, transmitted, or absorbed. Think about a pair of sunglasses. If you hold the sunglasses in your hand, you can see light that reflects off the lenses. If you put the sunglasses on, you see light that is transmitted through the lenses. The lenses also absorb some light. That is why objects appear darker when seen through the lenses.

Vocabulary

- transparent • translucent • opaque • primary color
- secondary color • complementary color • pigment

Skills

↻ Reading: Identify the Main Idea

△ Inquiry: Predict

Classifying Materials Lenses, like all objects, are made of different materials. Most materials can be classified as transparent, translucent, or opaque based on what happens to light that strikes the material.

A material that transmits most of the light that strikes it is called **transparent.** Light passes through a transparent material without being scattered. This allows you to see clearly what is on the other side. Water, air, and clear glass are all transparent materials. In **Figure 1,** the window shown in the photo is partially fogged up by condensation. The center of the window, where the condensation has been wiped away, is transparent. The fogged-up part of the window is translucent. A **translucent** (trans LOO sunt) material scatters the light that passes through it. You can usually see something behind a translucent object, but the details are blurred. Wax paper and frosted glass are translucent materials.

A material that reflects or absorbs all of the light that strikes it is called **opaque** (oh PAYK). You cannot see through opaque materials because light cannot pass through them. In **Figure 1,** the wood and snow shown in the photo are opaque. Metals and tightly woven fabric are other examples of opaque materials.

✎ **Identify the Main Idea**
Underline the main idea under the red heading Classifying Materials.

FIGURE 1 ·······

Types of Materials

The windows contain transparent, translucent, and opaque sections. ✎ **Relate Diagrams and Photos** Suppose the ball was placed behind the three-sectional window below. Draw what you would see inside the dashed circle.

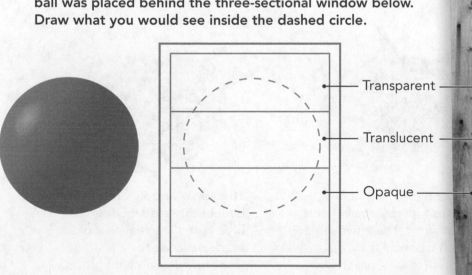

- Transparent
- Translucent
- Opaque

Vocabulary Prefixes How does knowing the meaning of the prefix *trans-* help you remember what happens to light that strikes a translucent object?

_____

_____

_____

_____

Opaque Objects The color of an opaque object depends on the wavelengths of light that the object reflects. Every opaque object absorbs some wavelengths of light and reflects others. 🔑 **The color of an opaque object is the color of the light it reflects.** For example, look at the apple shown at the top of **Figure 2.** The apple appears red because it reflects red wavelengths of light. The apple absorbs the other colors of light. The leaf looks green because it reflects green light and absorbs the other colors.

Objects can appear to change color if you view them in a different color of light. In red light, the apple appears red because there is red light for it to reflect. But the leaf appears black because there is no green light to reflect. In green light, the leaf looks green but the apple looks black. And in blue light, both the apple and the leaf look black.

Transparent and Translucent Objects Materials that are transparent or translucent allow only certain colors of light to pass through them. They reflect or absorb the other colors. 🔑 **The color of a transparent or translucent object is the color of the light it transmits.** For example, when white light shines through transparent blue glass, the glass appears blue because it transmits blue light.

White light

FIGURE 2 ···

▷ VIRTUAL LAB **Color of an Opaque Object**
The color an apple appears to be depends on the color of the light that strikes it. ✏️ **Infer Circle the correct answers in the text below each apple.**

Red light

Green light

Blue light

The apple appears red because it (absorbs/reflects) red light. The leaves look black because they (absorb/reflect) red light.

The apple appears black because it (absorbs/reflects) green light. The leaves look green because they (absorb/reflect) green light.

The apple appears black because it (absorbs/reflects) blue light. The leaves look black because they (absorb/reflect) blue light.

Transparent or translucent materials are used to make color filters. For example, a red color filter is red because it allows only red light to pass through it. When you look at an object through a color filter, the color of the object may appear different than when you see the object in white light.

The lenses in sunglasses are often color filters. For example, lenses tinted yellow are yellow filters. When you put on those sunglasses, some objects appear to change color. The color you see depends on the color of the filter and on the color of the object as it appears in white light.

apply it!

Predict Imagine looking at the beach ball at the right through a red, green, or blue filter. Predict how each section of the beach ball would appear. In the diagrams below, label each section of the beach ball with its corresponding color.

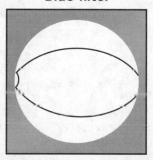

White light

Red filter	Green filter	Blue filter

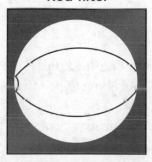

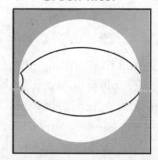

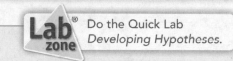

Lab zone ® Do the Quick Lab
Developing Hypotheses.

Assess Your Understanding

1a. Identify A(n) _____ object reflects or absorbs all the light that strikes it.

b. Apply Concepts A person wearing a blue shirt is standing in sunlight. What color(s) of light does the shirt reflect? What color(s) of light does the shirt absorb?

_____

_____

c. Predict Suppose you are wearing green-tinted glasses. What color would a blue shirt appear through these glasses? _____

got it?

○ **I get it!** Now I know that the color of an opaque object is _____

_____

and the color of a transparent or translucent object is _____

_____

○ **I need extra help with** _____

_____

Go to **MY SCIENCE** Ⓢ **COACH** *online for help with this subject.*

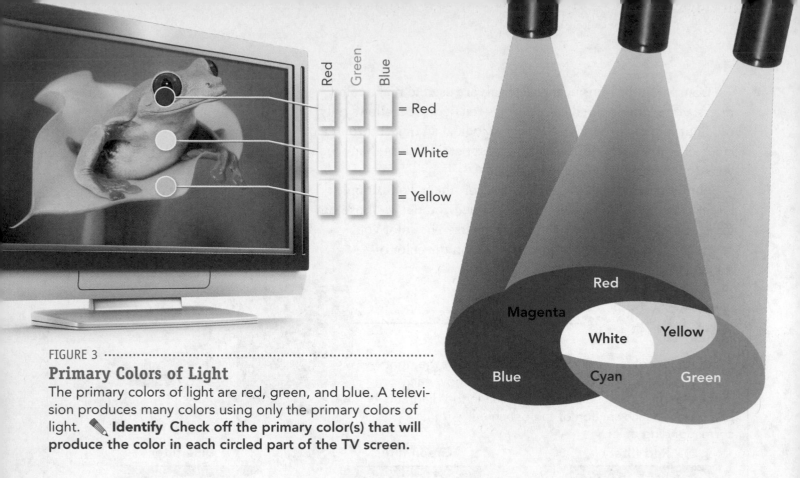

FIGURE 3

Primary Colors of Light
The primary colors of light are red, green, and blue. A television produces many colors using only the primary colors of light. ✎ **Identify** Check off the primary color(s) that will produce the color in each circled part of the TV screen.

How Do Colors Combine?

Color is used in painting, photography, theater lighting, and printing. People who work with color must learn how to produce a wide range of colors using just a few basic colors. Three colors that can combine to make any other color are called **primary colors.** Two primary colors combine in equal amounts to produce a **secondary color.**

Mixing Light The primary colors of light are red, green, and blue. 🔑 **When the three primary colors of light are combined in equal amounts, they produce white light.** If they are combined in different amounts, the primary colors can produce other colors. For example, red and green combine to form yellow light. Yellow is a secondary color of light because two primary colors produce it. The secondary colors of light are yellow (red + green), cyan (green + blue), and magenta (red + blue). **Figure 3** shows the primary and secondary colors of light.

A primary and a secondary color can combine to make white light. Any two colors that combine to form white light are called **complementary colors.** Yellow and blue are complementary colors, as are cyan and red, and magenta and green.

A television produces many colors using only the primary colors of light. The picture on a TV screen is made up of little bars of red, green, and blue light. By varying the brightness of each colored bar, the television can produce thousands of different colors.

Mixing light
List at least three examples of mixing light.

_____

_____

_____

_____

_____

_____

Mixing Pigment

Mixing Pigment How does an artist produce the many shades of colors you see in a painting? Inks, paints, and dyes contain **pigments,** or colored substances that are used to color other materials. Pigments absorb some colors and reflect others. The color you see is the result of the colors that a particular pigment reflects.

Mixing colors of pigments is different from mixing colors of light. As pigments are added together, fewer colors of light are reflected and more are absorbed. The more pigments that are combined, the darker the mixture looks.

Cyan, yellow, and magenta are the primary colors of pigments. **When the three primary colors of pigments are combined in equal amounts, they produce black.** By combining pigments in varying amounts, you can produce many other colors. If you combine two primary colors of pigments, you get a secondary color, as shown in **Figure 4.** The secondary colors of pigments are red, green, and blue.

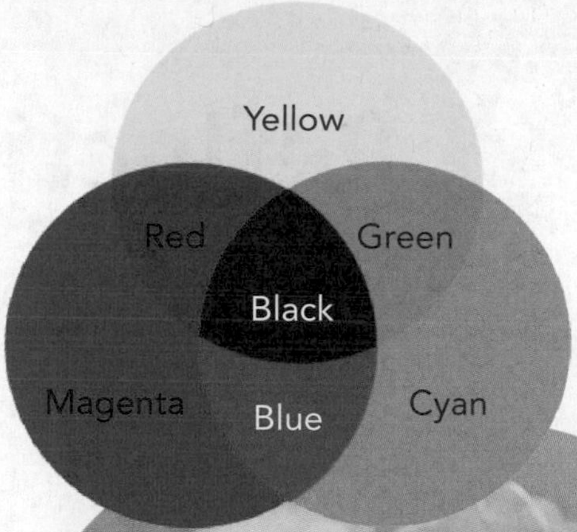

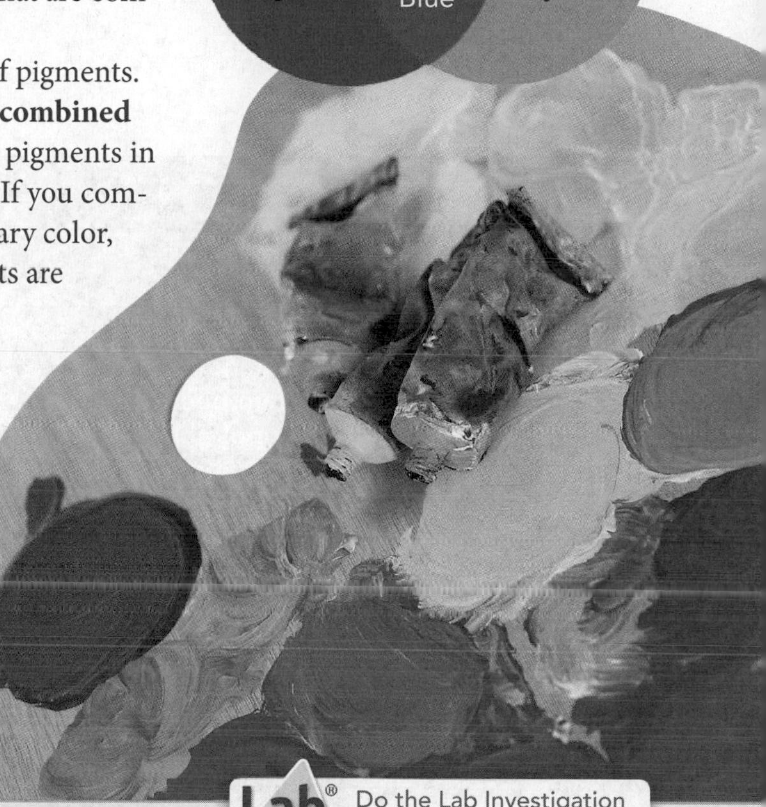

FIGURE 4 ....

Primary Colors of Pigment

Oil painters use a tray called a *palette* to hold and mix pigments. ✏️ **Identify** Write the names of the primary colors that combine to produce the secondary color at the end of each statement.

_____ + _____ = red

_____ + _____ = green

_____ + _____ = blue

Lab zone Do the Lab Investigation *Changing Colors.*

🔑 Assess Your Understanding

2a. Identify What are the primary colors of light? What are the primary colors of pigment?

_____

_____

_____

_____

b. Compare and Contrast The result of mixing the primary colors of light in equal amounts is the color _____. The result of mixing the primary colors of pigment in equal amounts is the color _____.

got it? ....

○ I get it! Now I know that to produce white light you combine _____

_____

○ I need extra help with _____

Go to my science **coach** *online for help with this subject.*

Reflection and Mirrors

UNLOCK THE BIG ?

What Are the Kinds of Reflection?

What Types of Images Do Mirrors Produce?

my planet diary

DISCOVERY

Periscope

In a submarine hidden beneath the ocean's surface, a captain peered into a long tube to see possible threats in the sea and air above. This sight tube, called a periscope, was designed by the Frenchman Marie Davey in 1854. Davey's periscope contained two mirrors, one placed at each end of a vertical tube. The mirrors were set parallel to each other and at 45 degrees to the vertical. The reflective surfaces faced each other. When light from an object on the surface reflected downward, an image appeared to the eye. People in submerged submarines could see what was above them!

Write your answer to the question below.

Imagine you are in a submerged submarine looking through a periscope. What are some things you might see?

_____

_____

_____

_____

_____

▶ PLANET DIARY Go to **Planet Diary** to learn more about mirrors.

Lab zone® Do the Inquiry Warm-Up
How Does Your Reflection Wink?

What Are the Kinds of Reflection?

Why do you see a reflection of yourself in a mirror but not on a page of your textbook? To answer this question, you need to understand how a surface reflects light. To show how light reflects, you can represent light waves as straight lines called **rays.** You may recall that light obeys the law of reflection—the angle of reflection equals the angle of incidence. 🔑 **The two ways in which a surface can reflect light are regular reflection and diffuse reflection.**

Vocabulary

- ray
- regular reflection
- image
- diffuse reflection
- plane mirror
- virtual image
- concave mirror
- optical axis
- focal point
- real image
- convex mirror

Skills

- Reading: Compare and Contrast
- Inquiry: Classify

Regular reflection occurs when parallel rays of light hit a smooth surface. All of the light rays reflect at the same angle because of the smooth surface. So you see a clear image. An **image** is a copy of the object formed by reflected or refracted rays of light. Shiny surfaces such as metal, glass, and calm water produce regular reflection.

Diffuse reflection occurs when parallel rays of light hit an uneven surface. Each light ray obeys the law of reflection but hits the surface at a different angle because the surface is uneven. Therefore, each ray reflects at a different angle. You either don't see an image or the image is not clear. Most objects reflect light diffusely. This is because most surfaces are not smooth. Even surfaces that appear to be smooth, such as a piece of paper, have small bumps that reflect light at different angles.

FIGURE 1 ·

Diffuse and Regular Reflection

✏ **Identify** Label the kind of reflection that occurs on each surface.

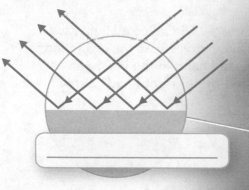

Lab zone® Do the Quick Lab *Observing.*

☞ Assess Your Understanding

got it? ·

○ **I get it!** Now I know the two kinds of reflection are_____

_____

○ **I need extra help with** _____

Go to MY SCIENCE ⑤ COACH online for help with this subject.

What Types of Images Do Mirrors Produce?

Have you ever looked at yourself in the curved mirrors of a fun house? If so, you know that your image looks different than it does in a flat mirror. Your image may look tall and skinny at one point and short and wide at another point. To understand why your image changes, you need to learn about the types of mirrors.

Plane Mirror Did you look into a mirror this morning to brush your teeth? If you did, you probably used a plane mirror. A **plane mirror** is a flat sheet of glass that has a smooth, silver-colored coating on one side. Often this coating is on the back of the glass to protect it from damage. When light strikes a mirror, the coating reflects the light. Because the coating is smooth, regular reflection occurs and a clear image forms. The image you see in a plane mirror is a **virtual image**—an image that forms where light seems to come from. "Virtual" describes something that does not really exist. Your image appears to be behind the mirror, but you can't reach behind the mirror and touch it.

🔑 **A plane mirror produces a virtual image that is upright and the same size as the object.** But the image is not quite the same as the object. The left and right of the image are reversed. For example, when you look in a mirror, your right hand appears to be a left hand in the image.

FIGURE 2 ···

Image in a Plane Mirror
A plane mirror forms a virtual image. The reflected light rays appear to come from behind the mirror, where the image forms.

✏️ **Interpret Photos** Is the raised hand in the image an image of the dancer's left hand or her right hand? Explain.

_____

_____

Image   Plane mirror   Object

Plane Mirror

Pretend your friend has never seen her image in a plane mirror. How would you describe to her the similarities and differences between her image and the real her?

_____

_____

_____

_____

_____

_____

_____

_____

Concave Mirrors

Concave Mirrors A mirror with a surface that curves inward like the inside of a bowl is a **concave mirror.** **Figure 3** shows how a concave mirror can reflect parallel rays of light so that they meet at a point. Notice that the rays of light shown are parallel to the optical axis. The **optical axis** is an imaginary line that divides a mirror in half, much like the equator that divides Earth into northern and southern halves. The point at which rays parallel to the optical axis reflect and meet is called the **focal point.**

The type of image that is formed by a concave mirror depends on the location of the object. ⟳ **Concave mirrors can produce real or virtual images.** A **real image** forms when light rays actually meet. If the object is farther away from the mirror than the focal point, the reflected rays form a real image. Unlike a virtual image, a real image can be projected on a surface such as a piece of paper. Real images are upside down. A real image may be smaller, larger, or the same size as the object.

If an object is between the mirror and the focal point, the reflected rays form a virtual image. Virtual images formed by a concave mirror are always larger than the object. Concave mirrors produce the magnified images you see in a makeup mirror.

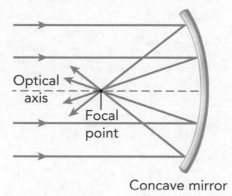

FIGURE 3 ·····
Concave Mirror
A concave mirror reflects rays of light parallel to the optical axis back through the focal point. The figures below show how a concave mirror can produce both real and virtual images.

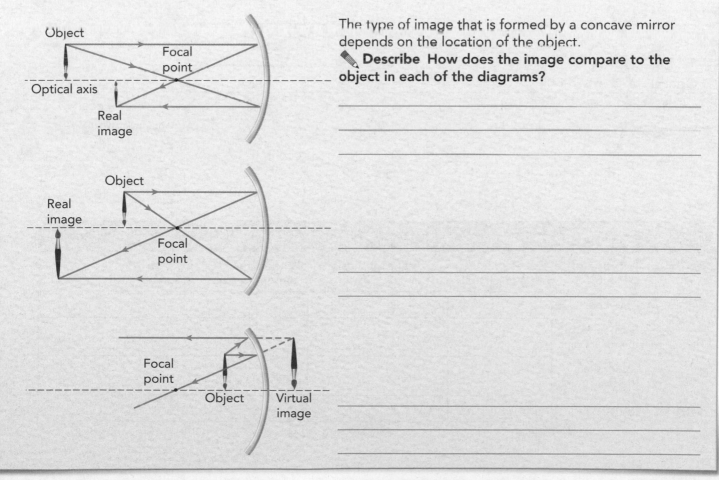

The type of image that is formed by a concave mirror depends on the location of the object.

✎ **Describe** How does the image compare to the object in each of the diagrams?

_____

_____

_____

_____

_____

_____

_____

_____

_____

_____

107

Compare and Contrast

Compare and contrast the shape of a convex mirror and a concave mirror.

_____

_____

_____

_____

Convex Mirrors

A mirror with a surface that curves outward is called a **convex mirror.** **Figure 4a** shows how convex mirrors reflect parallel rays of light. The reflected rays spread out but appear to come from a focal point behind the mirror. The focal point of a convex mirror is the point from which the rays appear to come. 🔑 **A convex mirror produces a virtual image that is always smaller than the object.**

Perhaps you have seen this warning on a car mirror: "Objects in mirror are closer than they appear." Convex mirrors are used in cars as passenger-side mirrors. The advantage of a convex mirror is that it allows you to see a larger area than you can with a plane mirror. The disadvantage is that the image is reduced in size. As a result, the image appears to be farther away than it actually is. The driver must understand this and adjust for it.

FIGURE 4 ....

> **INTERACTIVE ART** **Convex Mirror**

a. Light rays parallel to the optical axis reflect as if they came from the focal point behind a convex mirror.

b. ✏️ **CHALLENGE** Extend the two reflected rays behind the mirror to where they intersect. This is the top of the virtual image. Draw the image.

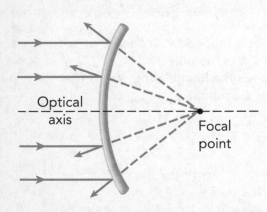

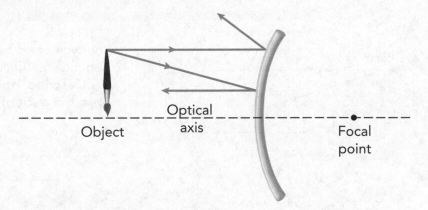

Complete the table to review the different types of images formed by mirrors.

Mirror	Location of Object	Is the image real or virtual?	Is the image upright or upside down?	What is the size of the image compared to the object?
Plane	Anywhere	_____	_____	_____
Concave	Farther than the focal point	_____	_____	_____
	Closer than the focal point	_____	_____	_____
Convex	Anywhere	_____	_____	_____

apply it!

Each of the photos shows an application of a curved mirror. A bus driver uses the mirror in the top photo to check for traffic. A boy uses the mirror in the bottom photo to put in contact lenses.

1 **Classify** Which type of curved mirror is in the top photo?_____

2 **Classify** Which type of curved mirror is in the bottom photo?_____

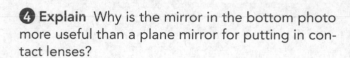

3 **Explain** Why is the mirror in the top photo more useful than a plane mirror for checking traffic?

_____

_____

_____

4 **Explain** Why is the mirror in the bottom photo more useful than a plane mirror for putting in contact lenses?

_____

_____

_____

 **Do the Quick Lab** *Mirror Images.*

🔑 Assess Your Understanding

1a. Define A(n) _____ is a copy of an object formed by reflected or refracted rays of light.

b. **Classify** A _____ mirror can form real and virtual images. _____ and _____ mirrors form only virtual images.

c. Apply Concepts Which type of mirror would you use if you wanted to project an image on a screen? Why?

_____

_____

_____

got it? ···

○ **I get it!** Now I know that the two types of images produced by mirrors are real _____

_____

○ **I need extra help with** _____

Go to **MY SCIENCE COACH** *online for help with this subject.*

Refraction and Lenses

🔑 **What Causes Light Rays to Bend?**

🔑 **What Determines the Type of Image Formed by a Lens?**

my planet diary

Isaac Newton

Sir Isaac Newton (1642–1727) may be best known as the man who came up with the theory of gravity. But Newton, who was born in England, made numerous other important contributions to both math and science, including defining the laws of motion and co-founding the field of calculus. In the 1660s, Newton investigated the laws of light and color. In his famous book *Opticks*, he describes how he passed sunlight through a prism to prove that white light consists of many colors. Newton was knighted in 1705 and was the first scientist to be buried at Westminster Abbey.

Communicate Write your answers to the questions below. Then discuss your answers with a partner.

1. How did Newton prove that sunlight consists of many colors?

_____

_____

2. Describe a discovery that you made through experimentation.

_____

_____

_____

_____

_____

> PLANET DIARY Go to **Planet Diary** to learn more about lenses.

 Do the Inquiry Warm-Up *How Can You Make an Image Appear?*

Vocabulary
- index of refraction • mirage • lens
- concave lens • convex lens

Skills
- ↻ Reading: Ask Questions
- △ Inquiry: Interpret Data

What Causes Light Rays to Bend?

A fish tank can play tricks on your eyes. If you look through the side of a fish tank, a fish seems closer than if you look at it from the top. If you look through the corner of the tank, you may see the same fish twice. Look at **Figure 1.** You see one image of the fish through the front of the tank and another through the side. The two images appear in different places! How can this happen?

Refraction can cause you to see something that may not actually be there. As you look at a fish in a tank, the light coming from the fish to your eye bends as it passes through three different mediums. The mediums are water, the glass of the tank, and air. As the light passes from one medium to the next, it is refracted. ⊙ **When light rays enter a new medium at an angle, the change in speed causes the rays to bend.**

FIGURE 1 ....

Optical Illusion in a Fish Tank

There is only one fish in this tank, but refraction makes it look as though there are two.

🖊 **Communicate** Discuss with a classmate some other examples of how the appearance of objects in water is different than in the air. Describe these examples below.

_____

_____

_____

_____

_____

_____

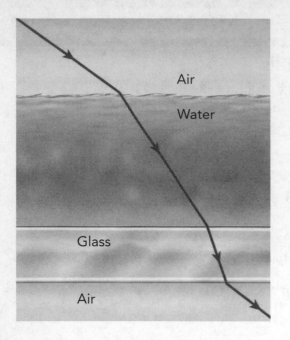

FIGURE 2
Refraction of Light
The light ray bends as it passes through different mediums.

✎ **Interpret Diagrams** In which medium does light travel the fastest?

_____

Refraction in Different Mediums
Some mediums cause light to bend more than others. **Figure 2** shows how the path of a light ray changes as it passes from one medium to another. When light passes from air into water, the light slows down. Light slows down again and bends even more when it passes from water into glass. When light passes from glass back into air, the light speeds up. Notice that the ray that leaves the glass is traveling in the same direction as it was before it entered the water. Light travels fastest in air, a little slower in water, and slower still in glass.

Glass causes light to bend more than either air or water does. Another way to say this is that glass has a higher index of refraction than either air or water. The **index of refraction** of a medium is a measure of how much a light ray bends when it enters that medium. The higher the index of refraction of a medium, the more it bends light. The index of refraction of water is 1.33. The index of refraction of glass is about 1.5. So light is bent more by glass than by water.

do the math! Analyzing Data

Bending Light

The table shows the index of refraction of some common mediums. **Use the data to answer the following questions.**

❶ ⚠ **Interpret Data** Which medium causes the greatest change in the direction of a light ray that enters at an angle?

_____

❷ ⚠ **Interpret Data** According to the table, which tend to bend light more, solids or liquids?

_____

❸ **Predict** Would you expect light to bend if it entered corn oil at an angle after it traveled through glycerol? Explain.

_____

_____

Index of Refraction	
Medium	**Index of Refraction**
Air (gas)	1.00
Water (liquid)	1.33
Ethyl alcohol (liquid)	1.36
Quartz (solid)	1.46
Corn oil (liquid)	1.47
Glycerol (liquid)	1.47
Glass, crown (solid)	1.52
Sodium chloride (solid)	1.54
Zircon (solid)	1.92
Diamond (solid)	2.42

Prisms and Rainbows Recall that when white light enters a prism, each wavelength is refracted by a different amount. The longer the wavelength, the less the wave is bent by a prism. Red, with the longest wavelength, is refracted the least. Violet, with the shortest wavelength, is refracted the most. This difference in refraction causes white light to spread out into the colors of the spectrum—red, orange, yellow, green, blue, and violet.

The same process occurs in water droplets suspended in the air. When white light from the sun shines through the droplets, a rainbow may appear. The water droplets act like tiny prisms, refracting and reflecting the light and separating the colors.

EXPLORE THE BIG Q?

Water + Light = A Rainbow

How does light interact with matter?
FIGURE 3 ···

> ART IN MOTION

A rainbow forms when light is reflected and refracted by water droplets suspended in the air. The diagram shows the path of a light ray that strikes a water droplet. ✎ **Interpret Diagrams** Use the diagram to answer the questions.

What happens to each color of light at point B?
_____
_____
_____
_____

Why does light separate out into its colors at point A?
_____
_____
_____
_____

A

B

C

Water droplet

What happens to each color of light at point C?
_____
_____
_____

_____

_____

_____

FIGURE 4 ·····························

Mirage
The puddles and reflections on the road are mirages.

Mirages You're traveling in a car on a hot day, and you notice that the road ahead looks wet. Yet when you get there, the road is dry. Did the puddles dry up? No, the puddles were never there! You saw a **mirage** (mih RAHJ)—an image of a distant object caused by refraction of light. The puddles on the road are light rays from the sky that are refracted to your eyes.

Figure 4 shows a mirage. Notice that there appears to be a reflection of the truck in the road. The air just above the road is hotter than the air higher up. Light travels faster in hot air. So light rays from the truck that travel toward the road are bent upward by the hot air. Your brain assumes that these rays traveled in a straight line. So the rays look as if they have reflected off a smooth surface. What you see is a mirage.

Lab zone Do the Quick Lab *Bent Pencil*.

🔑 Assess Your Understanding

1a. Identify A material's _____ is a measure of how much a ray of light bends when it enters that material from air.

b. Predict If a glass prism were in a medium with the same index of refraction, would it separate white light into different colors? Explain.

_____

_____

_____

c. ANSWER THE BIG ? How does light interact with matter?

_____

_____

_____

_____

_____

_____

_____

got it? ·····························

○ **I get it!** Now I know that the reason light rays bend when they enter a new medium at an angle is because _____

○ **I need extra help with** _____

Go to MY SCIENCE ⓢ COACH *online for help with this subject.*

What Determines the Type of Image Formed by a Lens?

Any time you look through binoculars, a camera, or eyeglasses, you are using lenses to bend light. A **lens** is a curved piece of glass or other transparent material that refracts light. A lens forms an image by refracting light rays that pass through it. Like mirrors, lenses can have different shapes. 🔑 **The type of image formed by a lens depends on the shape of the lens and the position of the object.**

Concave Lenses A concave lens is thinner in the center than at the edges. When light rays traveling parallel to the optical axis pass through a concave lens, they bend away from the optical axis and never meet. A concave lens can produce only virtual images because parallel light rays passing through the lens never meet.

Look at the book to the right. Notice that the words seen through the lens appear smaller than the words outside of the lens. The words seen through the lens are virtual images. A concave lens always produces a virtual image that is upright and smaller than the object. **Figure 5a** shows how a concave lens forms an image. The image is located where the light rays appear to come from.

FIGURE 5 ··

Concave Lens

a. A concave lens produces a virtual image that is upright and smaller than the object.

Object — Focal point — Image — Focal point

b. ✎ **Apply Concepts** Locate this object's image. Extend the two light rays straight back to the same side of the lens as the object. The point where they intersect is the location of the image. Draw the image.

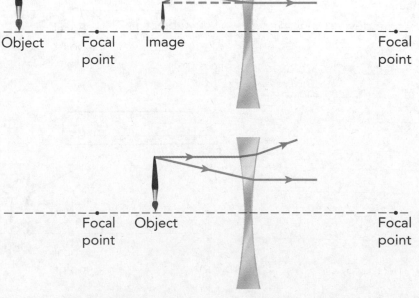

Focal point — Object — Focal point

115

Convex Lenses

Convex Lenses A **convex lens** is thicker in the center than at the edges. As light rays parallel to the optical axis pass through a convex lens, they are bent toward the center of the lens. The rays meet at the focal point of the lens and continue to travel beyond. The more curved the lens, the more it refracts light. A convex lens acts like a concave mirror, because it focuses rays of light.

An object's position relative to the focal point determines whether a convex lens forms a real or virtual image. Look at **Figure 6.** Notice that the words seen through the lens are larger than the words outside of the lens. The words seen through the lens are virtual images. When an object is between the lens and the focal point, the refracted rays form a virtual image. The image forms on the same side of the lens as the object and is larger than the object. If the object is outside of the focal point, the refracted rays form a real image on the other side of the lens. The real image can be smaller, larger, or the same size as the object. The diagrams in **Figure 7** show how a convex lens forms real and virtual images.

FIGURE 6 ···

Convex Lens

When an object is inside the focal point, the image seen through a convex lens is larger than the object. ✎ **Identify** Name a device that uses this type of lens.

_____

_____

Lenses

List some devices that use lenses.

_____

_____

_____

_____

_____

_____

FIGURE 7 ···

▶ **INTERACTIVE ART** **How a Convex Lens Works**

The type of image formed by a convex lens depends on the object's position. ✎ **Classify** Label which image is virtual and which image is real.

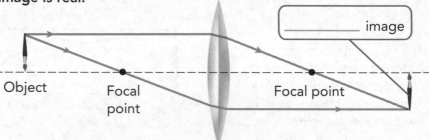

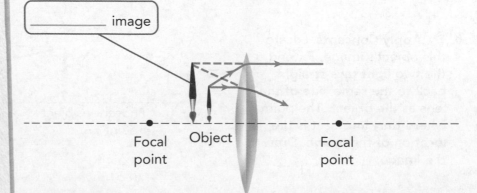

apply it!

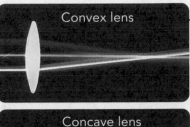
Convex lens

Concave lens

1 Interpret Photos These photos show parallel rays of light passing through a convex lens and a concave lens. Why do you suppose a convex lens is called a converging lens and a concave lens is called a diverging lens?

_____

_____

_____

2 Review Complete the Lenses and Mirrors table. Use the table to answer Question 3.

3 Summarize A convex lens acts like a _____ mirror. A concave lens acts like a _____ mirror.

4 CHALLENGE Suppose a convex lens and a concave mirror are underwater. Compared to the way they work in air, which one do you expect will be more affected by the water? Why?

_____

_____

_____

_____

Lenses and Mirrors

Type of Mirror or Lens	Real, Virtual, or Both Types of Images	Upright, Inverted, or Both Types of Images
Concave Mirror	Both	
Convex Mirror		Upright
Concave Lens		
Convex Lens		

Lab zone® Do the Quick Lab *Looking at Images.*

🔑 Assess Your Understanding

2a. Define A _____ is a curved piece of glass or other transparent material that refracts light.

b. Compare and Contrast Describe the shapes of a concave lens and a convex lens.

_____

_____

_____

c. Make Generalizations Use **Figure 7** to explain how you can you tell whether a convex lens will produce a real or virtual image.

_____

_____

_____

_____

_____

got it? ....

○ **I get it!** Now I know that the type of image formed by a lens depends on _____

_____

○ **I need extra help with** _____

Go to MY SCIENCE ⓢ COACH *online for help with this subject.*

Seeing Light

How Do You See Objects?

my planet Diary

Misconception: You can see in total darkness as long as your eyes adjust to the darkness.

Fact: It is impossible to see objects in total darkness. If there is some light, such as light from a street lamp or moonlight, we can see objects because the light reflects off the objects and enters our eyes. In these low light conditions, our eyes adjust to let more light in. It can take 10 to 30 minutes for this to happen.

Evidence: If a person is in a completely dark environment, such as a deep cave, he or she cannot see objects.

MISCONCEPTION

Communicate Write your answers to the questions below. Then discuss your answers with a partner.

1. How do you suppose your eyes adjust to let in more light?

_____

_____

_____

2. Think of an experiment to test whether or not humans can see in complete darkness.

_____

_____

_____

_____

> **PLANET DIARY** Go to **Planet Diary** to learn more about the human eye.

Do the Inquiry Warm-Up *Can You See Everything With One Eye?*

Vocabulary

- cornea • pupil • iris • retina • rods • cones
- optic nerve • nearsighted • farsighted

Skills

↺ **Reading:** Sequence

△ **Inquiry:** Observe

How Do You See Objects?

The first rule of baseball or softball is to keep your eye on the ball. As the ball moves near or far, your eyes must adjust continuously to keep it in focus. Fortunately, your eyes can change focus automatically. The eye is a complex structure with many parts. Each part plays a role in vision. ⚷ **You see objects when a process occurs that involves both your eyes and your brain.**

Light Enters the Eye Light enters the eye through the transparent front surface called the **cornea** (KAWR nee uh). The cornea protects the eye. It also acts as a lens to help focus light rays.

After passing through the cornea, light enters the pupil, the part of the eye that looks black. The **pupil** is an opening through which light enters the inside of the eye. In dim light, the pupil becomes larger to allow in more light. In bright light, the pupil becomes smaller to allow in less light. The **iris** is a ring of muscle that contracts and expands to change the size of the pupil. The iris gives the eye its color. In most people the iris is brown; in others it is blue, green, or hazel.

apply it!

The photographs show the same pupil exposed to different amounts of light.

❶ **Identify** Label which pupil is in dim light and which pupil is in bright light.

❷ **Explain** Why does the size of the pupil change?

_____

_____

❸ △**Observe** Work with a classmate. Cover one of your eyes with your hand for several seconds. Then remove your hand. Your classmate should observe what happens to your pupil. Switch roles. Record your observations.

_____

_____

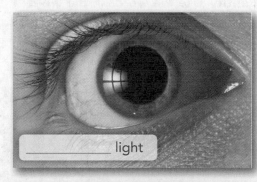

_____ light

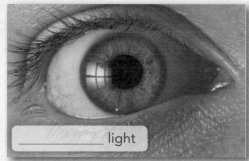

_____ light

Sequence A sequence is the order in which the steps in a process occur. As you read, complete the flowchart to show how you see objects.

How You See Objects

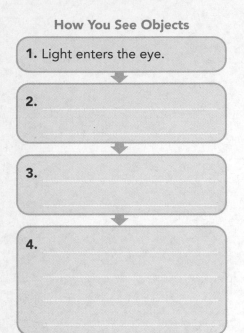

1. Light enters the eye.

2. _____

3. _____

4. _____

An Image Forms

After entering the pupil, the light passes through the lens. The lens is a convex lens that refracts light to form an image on the lining of your eyeball. Muscles, called ciliary muscles, hold the lens in place behind the pupil. When you focus on a distant object, the ciliary muscles relax, and the lens becomes longer and thinner. When you focus on a nearby object, the muscles contract, and the lens becomes shorter and fatter.

When the cornea and the lens refract light, an upside-down image is formed on the retina. The **retina** is a layer of cells that lines the inside of the eyeball. (Cells are the tiny structures that make up living things.) **Rods** are cells that contain a pigment that responds to small amounts of light. The rods allow you to see in dim light. **Cones** are cells that respond to color. They may detect red light, green light, or blue light. Cones respond best in bright light. Both rods and cones help change images on the retina into signals that then travel to the brain.

A Signal Goes to the Brain

The rods and cones send signals to the brain along a short, thick nerve called the **optic nerve.** The optic nerve begins at the blind spot, an area of the retina that has no rods or cones. Your brain interprets the signals from the optic nerve as an upright image. It also combines the two images from your eyes into a single three-dimensional image.

FIGURE 1 ·····························

The Human Eye

The human eye is a complex structure with many parts that allow you to see.

✏ **Identify** Use the words in the word bank to identify the parts of the eye.

Word Bank

Ciliary muscles
Cornea
Iris
Lens
Optic nerve
Pupil
Retina

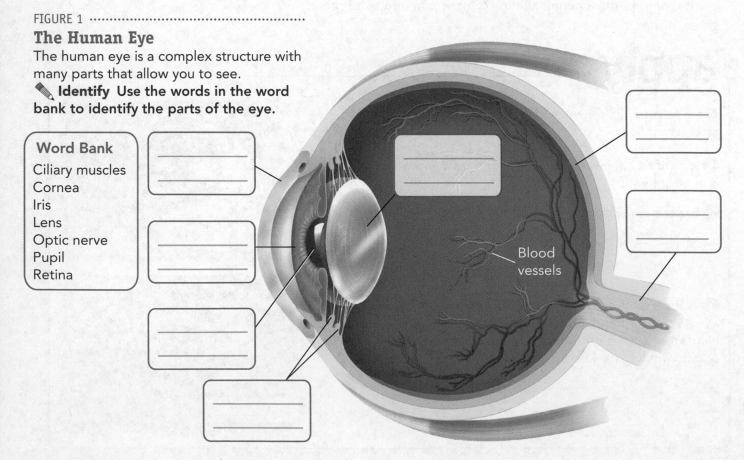

Blood vessels

Correcting Vision If the eyeball is slightly too long or too short, the image on the retina is out of focus. Fortunately, wearing glasses or contact lenses can correct this type of vision problem.

A **nearsighted** person can see nearby things clearly, but objects at a distance are blurred. The eyeball is too long, so the lens focuses the image in front of the retina. To correct this, a concave lens in front of the eye spreads out light rays before they enter the eye. As a result, the image forms on the retina.

A **farsighted** person can see distant objects clearly, but nearby objects appear blurry. The eyeball is too short, so the image that falls on the retina is out of focus. A convex lens corrects this by bending light rays toward each other before they enter the eye. An image then focuses on the retina.

 Diagnose the Patient! Read each patient's chart. Circle the diagnosis. Write in the type of lens needed in each case.

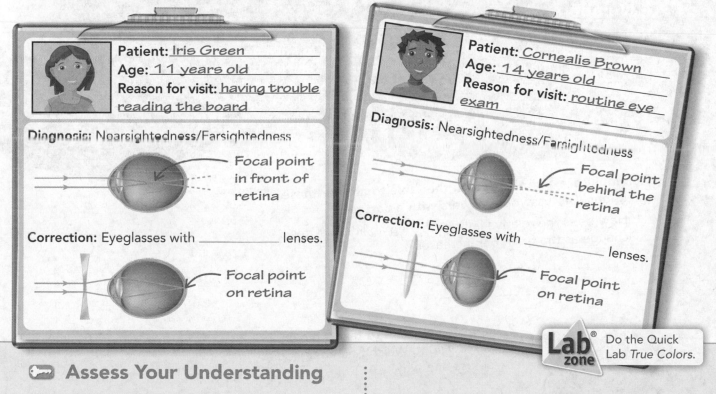

Patient: _Iris Green_

Age: _11 years old_

Reason for visit: _having trouble reading the board_

Diagnosis: Nearsightedness/Farsightedness

Focal point in front of retina

Correction: Eyeglasses with _____ lenses.

Focal point on retina

Patient: _Cornealis Brown_

Age: _14 years old_

Reason for visit: _routine eye exam_

Diagnosis: Nearsightedness/Farsightedness

Focal point behind the retina

Correction: Eyeglasses with _____ lenses.

Focal point on retina

Lab zone® Do the Quick Lab *True Colors.*

🔑 Assess Your Understanding

1a. Sequence The part of the eye that light enters first is called the _____

b. Explain How is an image formed on the retina?

_____

_____

_____

got it?

○ **I get it!** Now I know that seeing objects is a process that involves both _____

_____

○ **I need extra help with** _____

_____

Go to **MY SCIENCE** 💬 **COACH** *online for help with this subject.*

Using Light

UNLOCK
THE BIG
?

🔑 How Do Cameras, Telescopes, and Microscopes Work?

my planeT DiaRY

SCIENCE STATS

F-Numbers

Have you ever seen numbers such as F1.0, F1.4, or F2.8 on the LCD screen of a digital camera? These numbers are called *f-numbers*. F-numbers tell the size of the lens opening on the camera. The larger the f-number is, the smaller the lens opening is. By changing the f-number, a photographer can change the amount of light the lens lets in. The table shows the amount of light let in (relative ability to gather light) for different f-numbers.

Communicate Use the data in the table to answer these questions. Discuss your answers with a partner.

1. How does the relative light-gathering ability of a lens change as the f-number increases?

_____

_____

2. Suppose you want to take a picture in very low light. Which f-number would you use and why?

_____

_____

_____

F-number	Relative Ability to Gather Light
1.0	32×
1.4	16×
2.0	8×
2.8	4×
4.0	2×
5.6	1

> PLANET DIARY Go to **Planet Diary** to learn more about optical instruments.

 Lab zone ® Do the Inquiry Warm-Up *How Does a Pinhole Camera Work?*

Vocabulary
- camera • telescope • refracting telescope • objective
- eyepiece • reflecting telescope • microscope

Skills
- ↻ Reading: Relate Text and Visuals
- △ Inquiry: Infer

How Do Cameras, Telescopes, and Microscopes Work?

A microscope helps you see objects that are nearby. But another type of optical (or light-using) instrument, a telescope, helps you see objects that are far away. Three common types of optical instruments are cameras, telescopes, and microscopes.

Cameras A **camera** records an image of an object. A film camera records the image on film. A digital camera records the image electronically on a sensor. Both types of cameras follow the same basic principle. ⚿ **The lenses in a camera focus light to form a real, upside-down image in the back of the camera.** In many cameras, the lenses automatically move closer to or away from the film or sensor until the image is focused.

To take a photo with a digital camera, you press halfway down on a button called the shutter release. The camera automatically adjusts the amount of light that hits the sensor by changing the size of its opening. The camera also adjusts the amount of time that the sensor is exposed to light. When you press all the way down on the shutter release, the camera records the final image. The camera stores the final images so that you can transfer them to a computer.

apply it!

The diagram shows the structure of a digital camera.

❶ Interpret Diagrams What happens to each light ray as it passes through the lenses?

_____

❷ Identify On what part of the camera does an image form?

_____

❸ △ Infer Draw the image of the tree in the box to the right.

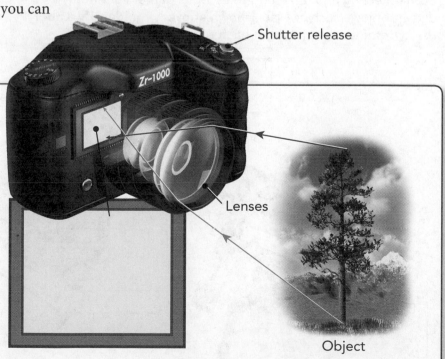

Shutter release

Lenses

Object

 Relate Text and Visuals
What is the purpose of the eyepiece in both types of telescopes and the microscope?
○ to shrink the image
○ to magnify the image
○ to gather light
○ to reflect light

Telescopes Distant objects are difficult to see because light from them has spread out by the time it reaches your eyes. Your eyes are too small to gather much light. A telescope forms enlarged images of distant objects. Telescopes use lenses or mirrors to collect and focus light from distant objects. The most common use of telescopes is to study objects in space.

Figure 1 shows the two main types of telescopes: refracting telescopes and reflecting telescopes. A refracting telescope consists of two convex lenses, one at each end of a tube. The larger lens is called the objective. The objective gathers the light coming from an object and focuses the rays to form a real image. The convex lens close to your eye is called the eyepiece. The eyepiece magnifies the image so you can see it clearly. The image seen through the refracting telescope is upside down.

A reflecting telescope uses a large concave mirror to gather light. The mirror collects light from distant objects and focuses the rays to form a real image. A small, plane mirror inside the telescope reflects the image to the eyepiece. The images you see through a reflecting telescope are upside down, just like the images seen through a refracting telescope.

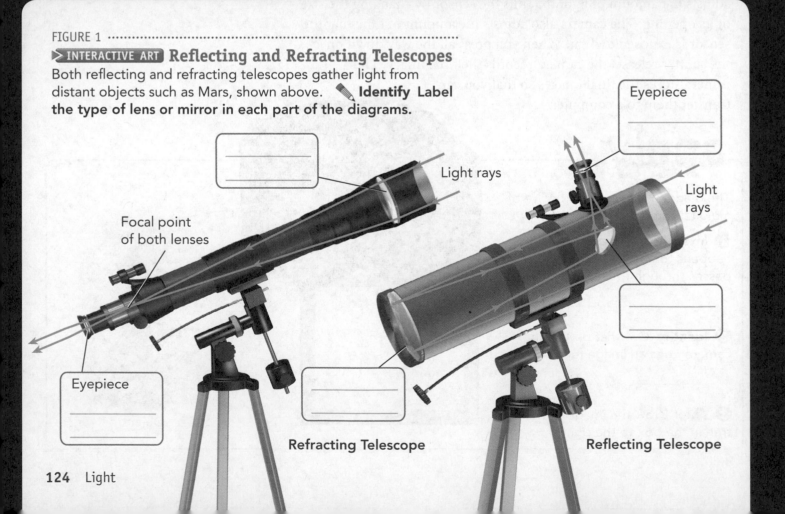

FIGURE 1

> INTERACTIVE ART **Reflecting and Refracting Telescopes**
Both reflecting and refracting telescopes gather light from distant objects such as Mars, shown above. **Identify** Label the type of lens or mirror in each part of the diagrams.

Eyepiece

Light rays

Focal point of both lenses

Eyepiece

Light rays

Refracting Telescope

Reflecting Telescope

Microscopes

To look at small, nearby objects, you would use a microscope. A **microscope** forms enlarged images of tiny objects. 🔑 **A microscope uses a combination of lenses to produce and magnify an image.** For example, the microscope that is shown in **Figure 2** uses two convex lenses to magnify an object, or specimen. The specimen is placed near the objective. The objective forms a real, enlarged image of the specimen. Then the eyepiece enlarges the image even more.

FIGURE 2 ·······································

Microscope

This microscope uses a combination of lenses to form enlarged images of tiny objects.

✏️ **CHALLENGE** The objects below have been enlarged by a microscope. Try to guess what they are. *(The answers are upside down below.)*

Eyepiece (convex lens)

Light rays

Objective (convex lens)

Slide with specimen

Light source

From left to right: human hair, leaf, insect (louse)

 Do the Quick Lab *What a View!*

🔑 Assess Your Understanding

1a. Review A _____ forms enlarged images of distant objects. A _____ forms enlarged images of tiny objects. A _____ records an image of an object.

b. Classify A pair of binoculars has two lenses in each tube. Which type of optical instrument are the binoculars most similar to?

_____

_____

_____

got it? ···

○ **I get it!** Now I know that telescopes, microscopes, and cameras use _____

_____

○ **I need extra help with** _____

Go to **MY SCIENCE COACH** online for help with this subject.

125

REVIEW THE BIG Q

When light interacts with matter, it can be _____ , _____ , or _____ .

LESSON 1 Light and Color

🔑 The color of an opaque object is the color of the light it reflects. The color of a transparent or translucent object is the color of the light it transmits.

🔑 When the three primary colors of light are combined in equal amounts, they produce white light. When the three primary colors of pigment are combined in equal amounts, they produce black.

Vocabulary
• transparent • translucent • opaque • primary color
• secondary color • complementary color • pigment

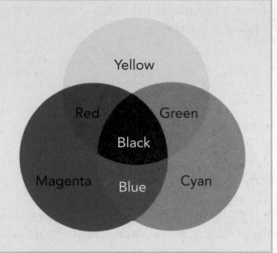

LESSON 2 Reflection and Mirrors

🔑 The two ways in which a surface can reflect light are regular reflection and diffuse reflection.

🔑 The three common types of mirrors are plane, concave, and convex.

Vocabulary
• ray • regular reflection • image
• diffuse reflection • plane mirror
• virtual image • concave mirror
• optical axis • focal point
• real image • convex mirror

LESSON 3 Refraction and Lenses

🔑 When light rays enter a new medium at an angle, the change in speed causes them to bend.

🔑 The type of image formed by a lens depends on the shape of the lens and the position of the object.

Vocabulary
• index of refraction • mirage • lens
• concave lens • convex lens

LESSON 4 Seeing Light

🔑 You see objects when a process occurs that involves both your eyes and your brain.

Vocabulary
• cornea • pupil • iris • retina
• rods • cones • optic nerve
• nearsighted • farsighted

LESSON 5 Using Light

🔑 Three common optical instruments are cameras, telescopes, and microscopes.

Vocabulary
• camera • telescope
• refracting telescope
• objective • eyepiece
• reflecting telescope
• microscope

Review and Assessment

LESSON 1 Light and Color

1. A type of material that reflects or absorbs all of the light that strikes it is called

  a. translucent.   **b.** transparent.

  c. reflective.   **d.** opaque.

2. Colors that combine to make any other color are called _____

3. Classify Do the colors shown below represent colors of pigments or light? Explain.

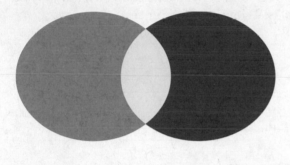

_____

_____

4. Compare and Contrast Why do you see the petals of a rose as red and the leaves as green? Explain.

_____

_____

_____

_____

_____

5. **Write About It** Helena works in the lighting crew for a theater. She needs to create a red spotlight on the stage. Kimi is a painter. He wants to create red paint for the background in a new painting. Use the terms *primary color* and *complementary color* to explain what color or combinations of colors each person must use. Explain any differences you note.

LESSON 2 Reflection and Mirrors

6. What type of reflection describes how light reflects off an uneven surface?

  a. real reflection   **b.** concave reflection

  c. diffuse reflection   **d.** regular reflection

7. Light rays obey the law of reflection, which states that _____

_____

_____

8. Draw Use a ruler to draw how the parallel light rays reflect off each mirror below.

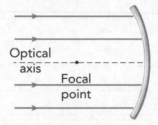

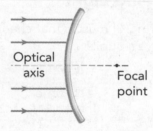

9. Classify Name the kind(s) of mirror(s) that can produce only virtual images.

_____

10. Apply Concepts Can a plane mirror produce a real image? Explain.

_____

_____

_____

_____

4 Review and Assessment

LESSON 3 Refraction and Lenses

11. A curved piece of glass or other transparent material that is used to refract light is called a

  a. prism.   **b.** lens.

  c. mirage.   **d.** mirror.

12. A _____ lens can produce only virtual images because parallel light rays passing through the lens never meet.

13. math! Quartz has an index of refraction of 1.46. Diamond has an index of refraction of 2.42. In which material does a light ray entering from air slow down more? Explain.

_____

_____

_____

_____

LESSON 4 Seeing Light

14. What is the ring of muscle that changes the size of the eye's pupil?

  a. iris   **b.** retina

  c. cornea   **d.** cone

15. A _____ person has trouble seeing things nearby.

16. Apply Concepts How are your eyes able to clearly see both near and distant objects?

_____

_____

_____

_____

_____

LESSON 5 Using Light

17. What is a device that helps you see very small, nearby objects more clearly?

  a. telescope   **b.** camera

  c. microscope   **d.** binoculars

18. A _____ telescope gathers light with a concave mirror.

19. Compare and Contrast How is a microscope similar to a convex lens used as a magnifying glass? How is it different?

_____

_____

_____

_____

_____

APPLY THE BIG ? How does light interact with matter?

20. Explain why the beam of light changes direction when it enters the water.

_____

_____

_____

_____

Standardized Test Prep

Multiple Choice

Circle the letter of the best answer.

1. The diagram below shows a periscope, a tool used to see objects not in the viewer's direct line of sight.

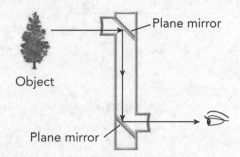

If you want to build a periscope, what measurement is most important?

A the width of the two mirrors

B the distance between the two mirrors

C the angle of the two mirrors

D the length of the tube

2. The index of refraction for water is 1.33 and for glass it is 1.5. What happens to the speed of light when light travels from glass into water?

A It increases.

B It decreases.

C It remains the same.

D It depends on the angle of incidence.

3. A convex lens can produce a real or a virtual image. Which type of mirror is most similar to a convex lens?

A concave mirror

B convex mirror

C plane mirror

D none of the above

4. You view an American flag through sunglasses that are tinted green. What colors do you see?

A green and blue

B red and black

C blue and red

D black and green

5. Which of the following describes looking at an object through a translucent material?

A You see the object clearly but it is upside down.

B You do not see the object at all.

C You see the object but its details are blurred.

D You see the object very clearly.

Constructed Response

Use the diagram below and your knowledge of science to help you answer Question 6. Write your answer on a separate sheet of paper.

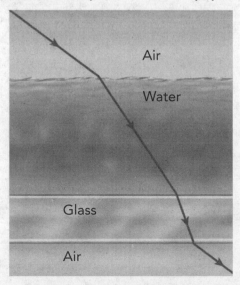

6. Explain why the path of the light ray changes as it travels through the different mediums.

Frontiers of Technology

Seeing Double

Lens

Light from star

Viewing mirror reflects light to eyepiece.

Concave mirror reflects light.

▲ Isaac Newton built the first model for a reflecting telescope in 1688.

Binoculars are really a set of two telescopes—one for each eye—that magnify distant objects. When scientists want to look at something even farther away, they can now turn to the world's largest pair of binoculars: the Large Binocular Telescope (LBT) on Mount Graham in Arizona.

The 120-million-dollar LBT is the world's most powerful optical telescope. It provides scientists with pictures and data of a huge area of space. The LBT has two massive mirrors that work together. Each mirror has a diameter of 8.4 meters! The mirrors gather light and allow scientists to look deeper into the universe than ever before. In fact, the LBT provides the same resolution as a 22.8-meter telescope—that's about as big as two school buses! It also has a larger field for collecting images than any single telescope, allowing scientists to see more.

Design It Research how mirrors work in a reflecting telescope. Make a model or draw a diagram of how a reflecting telescope works. Show how the angles of reflection would work with the mirrors placed at two different angles. Which angles will work best? Present your model or drawing to your class.

The world's largest binoculars peer into space. ▶

Hiding in Plain Sight

The South African dwarf chameleon has mastered the art of the quick change! This lizard can change the color of its skin in response to light, temperature, and other environmental factors.

Each of the four layers of the dwarf chameleon's skin plays a role in its brilliant appearance. The top layer is clear, so light passes right through it. The second layer has cells that contain a yellow pigment. The third layer doesn't have a specific color—it has cells that scatter light. The way these cells scatter light is similar to the way Earth's atmosphere scatters light, reflecting blue light especially well. The bottom layer of a dwarf chameleon's skin contains a pigment called melanin, which absorbs red light. Hormones control how the melanin is arranged in this layer. The melanin moves in response to light, temperature, and other environmental factors. As the melanin moves, the color of the chameleon's skin changes.

The chameleon's color results from the combination of the reflected light from the underlying layers of skin. When mostly blue light reflected from the third layer combines with light from the yellow layer, the chameleon is bright green.

The third layer of the dwarf chameleon's skin reflects blue light, which combines with the yellow in the second layer to make the chameleon appear bright green. ▼

Model It Use a piece of clear plastic wrap, yellow plastic wrap, a small prism, and white or blue paper to model the top three layers of the chameleon's skin. Does changing the angle of the prism change the color you see through the layers of "skin"? Draw a diagram of your model, and describe how changing the color of the bottom layer and the angle of the prism change the colors you see.

Safety Symbols

These symbols warn of possible dangers in the laboratory and remind you to work carefully.

 Safety Goggles Wear safety goggles to protect your eyes in any activity involving chemicals, flames or heating, or glassware.

 Lab Apron Wear a laboratory apron to protect your skin and clothing from damage.

 Breakage Handle breakable materials, such as glassware, with care. Do not touch broken glassware.

 Heat-Resistant Gloves Use an oven mitt or other hand protection when handling hot materials such as hot plates or hot glassware.

 Plastic Gloves Wear disposable plastic gloves when working with harmful chemicals and organisms. Keep your hands away from your face, and dispose of the gloves according to your teacher's instructions.

 Heating Use a clamp or tongs to pick up hot glassware. Do not touch hot objects with your bare hands.

 Flames Before you work with flames, tie back loose hair and clothing. Follow instructions from your teacher about lighting and extinguishing flames.

 No Flames When using flammable materials, make sure there are no flames, sparks, or other exposed heat sources present.

 Corrosive Chemical Avoid getting acid or other corrosive chemicals on your skin or clothing or in your eyes. Do not inhale the vapors. Wash your hands after the activity.

 Poison Do not let any poisonous chemical come into contact with your skin, and do not inhale its vapors. Wash your hands when you are finished with the activity.

 Fumes Work in a well-ventilated area when harmful vapors may be involved. Avoid inhaling vapors directly. Only test an odor when directed to do so by your teacher, and use a wafting motion to direct the vapor toward your nose.

 Sharp Object Scissors, scalpels, knives, needles, pins, and tacks can cut your skin. Always direct a sharp edge or point away from yourself and others.

 Animal Safety Treat live or preserved animals or animal parts with care to avoid harming the animals or yourself. Wash your hands when you are finished with the activity.

 Plant Safety Handle plants only as directed by your teacher. If you are allergic to certain plants, tell your teacher; do not do an activity involving those plants. Avoid touching harmful plants such as poison ivy. Wash your hands when you are finished with the activity.

 Electric Shock To avoid electric shock, never use electrical equipment around water, or when the equipment is wet or your hands are wet. Be sure cords are untangled and cannot trip anyone. Unplug equipment not in use.

 Physical Safety When an experiment involves physical activity, avoid injuring yourself or others. Alert your teacher if there is any reason you should not participate.

 Disposal Dispose of chemicals and other laboratory materials safely. Follow the instructions from your teacher.

 Hand Washing Wash your hands thoroughly when finished with an activity. Use soap and warm water. Rinse well.

 General Safety Awareness When this symbol appears, follow the instructions provided. When you are asked to develop your own procedure in a lab, have your teacher approve your plan before you go further.

Using a Laboratory Balance

The laboratory balance is an important tool in scientific investigations. You can use a balance to determine the masses of materials that you study or experiment with in the laboratory.

Different kinds of balances are used in the laboratory. One kind of balance is the triple-beam balance. The balance that you may use in your science class is probably similar to the balance illustrated in this Appendix. **To use the balance properly, you should learn the name, location, and function of each part of the balance you are using. What kind of balance do you have in your science class?**

The Triple-Beam Balance

The triple-beam balance is a single-pan balance with three beams calibrated in grams. The back, or 100-gram, beam is divided into ten units of 10 grams each. The middle, or 500-gram, beam is divided into five units of 100 grams each. The front, or 10-gram, beam is divided into ten units of 1 gram each. Each of the units on the front beam is further divided into units of 0.1 gram. What is the largest mass you could find with a triple-beam balance?

The following procedure can be used to find the mass of an object with a triple-beam balance:
1. Place the object on the pan.
2. Move the rider on the middle beam notch by notch until the horizontal pointer on the right drops below zero. Move the rider back one notch.
3. Move the rider on the back beam notch by notch until the pointer again drops below zero. Move the rider back one notch.
4. Slowly slide the rider along the front beam until the pointer stops at the zero point.
5. The mass of the object is equal to the sum of the readings on the three beams.

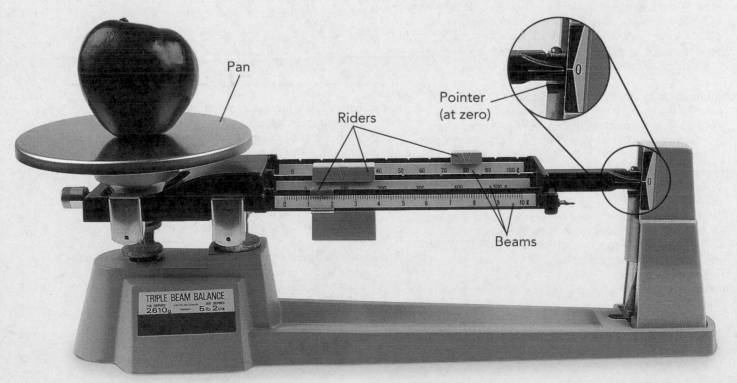

Pan

Riders

Pointer (at zero)

Beams

TRIPLE BEAM BALANCE
2610g   5 lb 2 oz

GLOSSARY

A

amplitude **1.** The height of a transverse wave from the center to a crest or trough. **2.** The maximum distance the particles of a medium move away from their rest positions as a longitudinal wave passes through the medium. (11)
amplitud **1.** Altura de una onda transversal desde el centro a una cresta o un valle. **2.** Máxima distancia del desvío de las partículas de un medio, desde sus posiciones de reposo, al ser atravesado por una onda longitudinal.

amplitude modulation A method of transmitting signals by changing the amplitude of a radio wave. (82)
amplitud modulada Método de transmisión de señales al cambiar la amplitud de una onda de radio.

antinode A point of maximum amplitude on a standing wave. (22)
antinodo Punto de máxima amplitud de una onda estacionaria.

C

camera An optical instrument that uses lenses to focus light, and film or an electronic sensor to record an image of an object. (123)
cámara Instrumento óptico que usa lentes para enfocar la luz, y película o un sensor electrónico para grabar la imagen de un objeto.

cochlea A snail-shaped tube in the inner ear that is lined with receptor cells that respond to sound. (52)
cóclea Conducto en forma de caracol del oído interno que está cubierto de células receptoras que responden al sonido.

complementary colors Any two colors that combine to form white light. (102)
colores complementarios Dos colores cualesquiera que se combinan para crear luz blanca.

compression **1.** Stress that squeezes rock until it folds or breaks. **2.** The part of a longitudinal wave where the particles of the medium are close together. (8)
compresión **1.** Fuerza que oprime una roca hasta que se pliegue o quiebre. **2.** Parte de una onda longitudinal en la que las partículas del medio están muy próximas unas con otras.

concave lens A lens that is thinner in the center than at the edges. (115)
lente cóncava Lente que es más fina en el centro que en los extremos.

concave mirror A mirror with a surface that curves inward. (107)
espejo cóncavo Espejo cuya superficie se curva hacia dentro.

cones Cells in the retina that respond to and detect color. (120)
conos Células en la retina que responden y detectan el color.

constructive interference The interference that occurs when two waves combine to make a wave with an amplitude larger than the amplitude of either of the individual waves. (20)
interferencia constructiva Interferencia que ocurre cuando se combinan ondas para crear una onda con una amplitud mayor a la de cualquiera de las ondas individuales.

convex lens A lens that is thicker in the center than at the edges. (116)
lente convexa Lente que es más gruesa en el centro que en los extremos.

convex mirror A mirror with a surface that curves outward. (108)
espejo convexo Espejo cuya superficie se curva hacia fuera.

cornea The transparent tissue that covers the front of the eye. (119)
córnea Tejido transparente que cubre la parte delantera del ojo.

crest The highest part of a transverse wave. (7)
cresta Parte más alta de una onda transversal.

D

decibel (dB) A unit used to compare the loudness of different sounds. (43)
decibelio (dB) Unidad usada para comparar el volumen de distintos sonidos.

density The ratio of the mass of a substance to its volume (mass divided by volume). (39)
densidad La razón de la masa de una sustancia por su volumen (la masa se divide por el volumen).

destructive interference The interference that occurs when two waves combine to make a wave with an amplitude smaller than the amplitude of either of the individual waves. (21)
interferencia destructiva Interferencia que ocurre cuando dos ondas se combinan para crear una onda con una amplitud menor a la de cualquiera de las ondas individuales.

diffraction The bending or spreading of waves as they move around a barrier or pass through an opening. (19)
difracción Desviación de las ondas al desplazarse alrededor de una barrera o atravesar una abertura.

diffuse reflection Reflection that occurs when parallel rays of light hit an uneven surface and all reflect at different angles. (105)
reflexión difusa Reflexión que ocurre cuando rayos de luz paralelos tocan una superficie rugosa y se reflejan en diferentes ángulos.

Doppler effect The change in frequency of a wave as its source moves in relation to an observer. (44)
efecto Doppler Cambio en la frecuencia de una onda a medida que la fuente se mueve en relación al observador.

E

ear canal A narrow region leading from the outside of the human ear to the eardrum. (52)
canal auditivo Región estrecha que conecta el exterior del oído humano con el tímpano.

eardrum The small, tightly stretched drumlike membrane that separates the outer ear from the middle ear, and that vibrates when sound waves strike it. (52)
tímpano Membrana pequeña extendida y tensa, como la de un tambor, que separa el oído externo del oído medio y que vibra al percibir ondas de sonido.

echolocation The use of reflected sound waves to determine distances or to locate objects. (55)
ecolocación Uso de ondas sonoras reflejadas para determinar distancias o para localizar objetos.

electromagnetic radiation The energy transferred through space by electromagnetic waves. (69)
radiación electromagnética Energía transferida por ondas electromagnéticas a través del espacio.

electromagnetic spectrum The complete range of electromagnetic waves placed in order of increasing frequency. (74)
espectro electromagnético Gama completa de ondas electromagnéticas organizadas de menor a mayor frecuencia.

electromagnetic waves Waves that can transfer electric and magnetic energy through the vacuum of space. (69)
ondas electromagnéticas Ondas que pueden transferir energía eléctrica y magnética a través del vacío del espacio.

energy The ability to do work or cause change. (5)
energía Capacidad para realizar un trabajo o producir cambios.

eyepiece A lens that magnifies the image formed by the objective. (124)
ocular Lente que aumenta la imagen formada por el objetivo.

F

farsighted Having the condition in which a person can see distant objects clearly and nearby objects as blurry. (121)
hipermetropía Condición en la que una persona ve con claridad los objetos lejanos y ve borrosos los objetos cercanos.

focal point The point at which light rays parallel to the optical axis meet, or appear to meet, after being reflected (or refracted) by a mirror (or a lens). (107)
punto de enfoque Punto en el que se encuentran, o parecen encontrarse, los rayos de luz paralelos al eje óptico después de reflejarse (o refractarse) en un espejo (o lente).

frequency The number of waves passing a given point each second. (12)
frecuencia Número de ondas que pasan por un punto dado cada segundo.

frequency modulation A method of transmitting signals by changing the frequency of a wave. (82)
frecuencia modulada Método de transmisión de señales mediante el cambio de la frecuencia de una onda.

fundamental tone The lowest natural frequency of an object. (47)
tono fundamental Frecuencia natural más baja de un cuerpo.

G

gamma rays Electromagnetic waves with the shortest wavelengths and highest frequencies. (78)
rayos gamma Ondas electromagnéticas con las longitudes de onda más cortas y las frecuencias más altas.

GLOSSARY

H

hertz (Hz) Unit of measurement for frequency. (12)
hercio (Hz) Unidad de medida de la frecuencia.

I

image A copy of an object formed by reflected or refracted rays of light. (105)
imagen Copia de un objeto formado por rayos de luz que se reflejan y se refractan.

index of refraction A measure of the amount a ray of light bends when it passes from one medium to another. (112)
índice de refracción Medida de la inclinación de un rayo de luz cuando pasa de un medio a otro.

infrared rays Electromagnetic waves with shorter wavelengths and higher frequencies than microwaves. (76)
rayos infrarrojos Ondas electromagnéticas con longitudes de onda más cortas y frecuencias más altas que las microondas.

intensity The amount of energy per second carried through a unit area by a wave. (42)
intensidad Cantidad de energía por segundo que transporta una onda a través de una unidad de área.

interference The interaction between waves that meet. (20)
interferencia Interacción entre dos o más ondas que se encuentran.

iris The ring of muscle that surrounds the pupil and regulates the amount of light entering the eye; gives the eye its color. (119)
iris Disco de músculo que rodea la pupila y regula la cantidad de luz que entra al ojo; da color al ojo.

L

lens **1.** The flexible structure that focuses light that has entered the eye. **2.** A curved piece of glass or other transparent material that is used to refract light. (115)
lente **1.** Estructura flexible que enfoca la luz que entra al ojo. **2.** Trozo curvo de vidrio u otro material transparente que se usa para refractar la luz.

longitudinal wave A wave that moves the medium in a direction parallel to the direction in which the wave travels. (8)
onda longitudinal Onda que mueve al medio en una dirección paralela a la dirección en la que se propaga la onda.

loudness Perception of the energy of a sound. (42)
volumen Percepción de la energía de un sonido.

M

mechanical wave A wave that requires a medium through which to travel. (5)
onda mecánica Onda que necesita un medio por el cual propagarse.

medium The material through which a wave travels. (5)
medio Material a través del cual se propaga una onda.

microscope An optical instrument that forms enlarged images of tiny objects. (125)
microscopio Instrumento óptico que forma imágenes aumentadas de objetos diminutos.

microwaves Electromagnetic waves that have shorter wavelengths and higher frequencies than radio waves. (75)
microondas Ondas electromagnéticas con longitudes de onda más cortas y frecuencias más altas que las ondas de radio.

mirage An image of a distant object caused by refraction of light as it travels through air of varying temperature. (114)
espejismo Imagen de un objeto distante causado por la refracción de la luz cuando viaja por el aire a temperaturas cambiantes.

music A set of sounds or notes combined in ways that are pleasing. (46)
música Conjunto de sonidos o notas que se combinan de una manera agradable.

N

nearsighted Having the condition in which a person can see nearby objects clearly and distant objects as blurry. (121)
miopía Condición en la que una persona ve con claridad los objetos cercanos y ve borrosos los objetos lejanos.

node A point of zero amplitude on a standing wave. (22)
nodo Punto de amplitud cero de una onda estacionaria.

O

objective A lens that gathers light from an object and forms a real image. (124)
objetivo Lente que reúne la luz de un objeto y forma una imagen real.

opaque A type of material that reflects or absorbs all of the light that strikes it. (99)
material opaco Material que refleja o absorbe toda la luz que llega a él.

optic nerve Short, thick nerve that carries signals from the eye to the brain. (120)
nervio óptico Nervio corto y grueso que lleva señales del ojo al cerebro.

optical axis An imaginary line that divides a mirror in half. (107)
eje óptico Recta imaginaria que divide un espejo por la mitad.

overtone A natural frequency that is a multiple of the fundamental tone's frequency. (47)
armónico Frecuencia natural que es un múltiplo de la frecuencia del tono fundamental.

P

photoelectric effect The ejection of electrons from a substance when light is shined on it. (71)
efecto fotoeléctrico Expulsión de electrones de una sustancia al ser iluminada.

photon A tiny particle or packet of light energy. (71)
fotón Partícula diminuta o paquete de energía luminosa.

pigment 1. A colored chemical compound that absorbs light. 2. A colored substance used to color other materials. (103)
pigmento 1. Compuesto químico de color que absorbe luz. 2. Sustancia de color que se puede usar para dar color a otros materiales.

pitch A description of how a sound is perceived as high or low. (40)
tono Descripción de un sonido que se percibe como alto o bajo.

plane mirror A flat mirror that produces an upright, virtual image the same size as the object. (106)
espejo plano Espejo liso que produce una imagen virtual vertical del mismo tamaño que el objeto.

polarized light Light that has been filtered so that all of its waves are parallel to each other. (70)
luz polarizada Luz que se ha filtrado de manera que sus ondas queden paralelas unas con otras.

primary color One of three colors that can be used to make any other color. (102)
color primario Uno de los tres colores que se pueden usar para hacer cualquier color.

pupil The opening in the center of the iris through which light enters the inside of the eye. (119)
pupila Apertura en el centro del iris por donde entra la luz al ojo.

R

radar A system that uses reflected radio waves to detect objects and measure their distance and speed. (75)
radar Sistema que usa ondas de radio reflejadas para detectar cuerpos y medir su distancia y velocidad.

radio waves Electromagnetic waves with the longest wavelengths and lowest frequencies. (74)
ondas de radio Ondas electromagnéticas con las longitudes de onda más largas y las frecuencias más bajas.

rarefaction The part of a longitudinal wave where the particles of the medium are far apart. (8)
rarefacción Parte de una onda longitudinal donde las partículas del medio están muy apartadas entre sí.

ray A straight line used to represent a light wave. (104)
rayo Línea recta que se usa para representar una onda de luz.

real image An upside-down image formed where rays of light meet. (107)
imagen real Imagen invertida formada en el punto de encuentro de los rayos de luz.

reflecting telescope A telescope that uses a curved mirror to collect and focus light. (124)
telescopio de reflexión Telescopio que usa un espejo curvado para captar y enfocar la luz.

GLOSSARY

reflection The bouncing back of an object or a wave when it hits a surface through which it cannot pass. (17)
reflexión Rebote de un cuerpo o una onda al golpear una superficie que no puede atravesar.

refracting telescope A telescope that uses convex lenses to gather and focus light. (124)
telescopio de refracción Telescopio que usa lentes convexas para captar y enfocar la luz.

refraction The bending of waves as they enter a new medium at an angle, caused by a change in speed. (18)
refracción Cambio de dirección de las ondas al entrar en un nuevo medio con un determinado ángulo, y a consecuencia de un cambio de velocidad.

regular reflection Reflection that occurs when parallel rays of light hit a smooth surface and all reflect at the same angle. (105)
reflexión regular Reflexión que ocurre cuando rayos de luz paralelos chocan contra una superficie lisa y se reflejan en el mismo ángulo.

resonance The increase in the amplitude of a vibration that occurs when external vibrations match an object's natural frequency. (23)
resonancia Aumento en la amplitud de vibración que ocurre cuando vibraciones externas corresponden con la frecuencia natural de un cuerpo.

retina The layer of receptor cells at the back of the eye on which an image is focused. (120)
retina Capa de células receptoras de la parte posterior del ojo donde se enfoca una imagen.

rods Cells in the retina that detect dim light. (120)
bastones Células de la retina que detectan la luz tenue.

————————— **S** —————————

secondary color Any color produced by combining equal amounts of any two primary colors. (102)
color secundario Color producido al combinar iguales cantidades de dos colores primarios cualesquiera.

sonar A system that uses reflected sound waves to locate and determine the distance to objects under water. (56)
sónar Sistema que usa ondas sonoras reflejadas para detectar y localizar objetos bajo agua.

sonogram An image formed using reflected ultrasound waves. (57)
sonograma Formación de una imagen usando ondas de ultrasonido reflejadas.

standing wave A wave that appears to stand in one place, even though it is two waves interfering as they pass through each other. (22)
onda estacionaria Onda que parece permanecer en un lugar, y que en realidad es la interferencia de dos ondas que se atraviesan.

————————— **T** —————————

telescope An optical instrument that forms enlarged images of distant objects. (124)
telescopio Instrumento óptico que forma imágenes aumentadas de los objetos lejanos.

thermogram An image that shows regions of different temperatures in different colors. (76)
termograma Imagen que muestra regiones de distintas temperaturas con distintos colores.

translucent A type of material that scatters light as it passes through. (99)
material traslúcido Material que dispersa la luz cuando ésta lo atraviesa.

transparent A type of material that transmits light without scattering it. (99)
material transparente Material que transmite luz sin dispersarla.

transverse wave A wave that moves the medium at right angles to the direction in which the wave travels. (7)
onda transversal Onda que desplaza a un medio perpendicularmente a la dirección en la que viaja la onda.

trough The lowest part of a transverse wave. (7)
valle Parte más baja de una onda transversal.

————————— **U** —————————

ultrasound Sound waves with frequencies above 20,000 Hz. (55)
ultrasonido Ondas sonoras con frecuencias mayores de 20,000 Hz.

ultraviolet rays (radiation) Electromagnetic waves with wavelengths shorter than visible light but longer than X-rays. (77)
rayos (radiación) ultravioleta Ondas electromagnéticas con longitudes de onda más cortas que la luz visible pero más largas que los rayos X.

V

vibration A repeated back-and-forth or up-and-down motion. (6)
vibración Movimiento repetido hacia delante y hacia atrás o hacia arriba y hacia abajo.

virtual image An upright image formed where rays of light appear to come from. (106)
imagen virtual Imagen vertical que se forma desde donde parecen provenir los rayos de luz.

visible light Electromagnetic radiation that can be seen with the unaided eye. (77)
luz visible Radiación electromagnética que se puede ver a simple vista.

W

wave **1**. A disturbance that transfers energy from place to place. **2**. The movement of energy through a body of water. (5)
onda **1**. Perturbación que transfiere energía de un lugar a otro. **2**. Desplazamiento de energía a través de un cuerpo de agua.

wavelength The distance between the crest of one wave and the crest of the next wave. (12)
longitud de onda Distancia entre la cresta de una onda y la cresta de la siguiente onda.

X

X-rays Electromagnetic waves with wavelengths shorter than ultraviolet rays but longer than gamma rays. (78)
rayos X Ondas electromagnéticas con longitudes de onda más cortas que los rayos ultravioleta pero más largas que los rayos gamma.

INDEX

Page numbers for key terms are printed in **boldface** type.

INDEX

Page numbers for key terms are printed in **boldface** type.

X

ACKNOWLEDGMENTS

Staff Credits

The people who made up the *Interactive Science* team—representing composition services, core design digital and multimedia production services, digital product development, editorial, editorial services, manufacturing, and production—are listed below.

Jan Van Aarsen, Samah Abadir, Ernie Albanese, Bridget Binstock, Suzanne Biron, MJ Black, Nancy Bolsover, Stacy Boyd, Jim Brady, Katherine Bryant, Michael Burstein, Pradeep Byram, Jessica Chase, Jonathan Cheney, Arthur Ciccone, Allison Cook-Bellistri, Rebecca Cottingham, AnnMarie Coyne, Bob Craton, Chris Deliee, Paul Delsignore, Michael Di Maria, Diane Dougherty, Kristen Ellis, Theresa Eugenio, Amanda Ferguson, Jorgensen Fernandez, Kathryn Fobert, Julia Gecha, Mark Geyer, Steve Gobbell, Paula Gogan-Porter, Jeffrey Gong, Sandra Graff, Adam Groffman, Lynette Haggard, Christian Henry, Karen Holtzman, Susan Hutchinson, Sharon Inglis, Marian Jones, Sumy Joy, Sheila Kanitsch, Courtenay Kelley, Chris Kennedy, Toby Klang, Greg Lam, Russ Lappa, Margaret LaRaia, Ben Leveillee, Thea Limpus, Dotti Marshall, Kathy Martin, Robyn Matzke, John McClure, Mary Beth McDaniel, Krista McDonald, Tim McDonald, Rich McMahon, Cara McNally, Melinda Medina, Angelina Mendez, Maria Milc`zarek`, Claudi Mimo, Mike Napieralski, Deborah Nicholls, Dave Nichols, William Oppenheimer, Jodi O'Rourke, Ameer Padshah, Lorie Park, Celio Pedrosa, Jonathan Penyack, Linda Zust Reddy, Jennifer Reichlin, Stephen Rider, Charlene Rimsa, Stephanie Rogers, Marcy Rose, Rashid Ross, Anne Rowsey, Logan Schmidt, Amanda Seldera, Laurel Smith, Nancy Smith, Ted Smykal, Emily Soltanoff, Cindy Strowman, Dee Sunday, Barry Tomack, Patricia Valencia, Ana Sofia Villaveces, Stephanie Wallace, Christine Whitney, Brad Wiatr, Heidi Wilson, Heather Wright, Rachel Youdelman

Photography

All uncredited photos copyright © 2011 Pearson Education.

Cover
Boy with horn, David Deas/DK Stock/Getty Images; **reflection,** Al Satterwhite/Tips Images.

Front Matter
Page vi, John Lund/Corbis; **vii,** Adam Hunger/AP Images; **viii,** Don Carstens/Robertstock; **ix,** *Cloud Gate*, Millennium Park, Chicago (2004), Anish Kapoor. Photo © 2008 Kim Karpeles; **xi laptop,** iStockphoto.com; **xiii bl,** JupiterImages/Getty Images; **xvi laptop,** iStockphoto.com; **xx–xxi spread,** Stockbyte/Getty Images.

Chapter 1
Pages xxii–1, John Lund/Corbis; **3 t,** Sami Sarkis/Photographer's Choice/Getty Images; **3 m,** Richard Megna/Fundamental Photographs, NYC; **3 b,** Richard Megna/Fundamental Photographs, NYC; **4** Wen Zhenxiao/ChinaFotoPress/Zuma Press; **5,** Adrian Lourie/Alamy; **6,** Sami Sarkis/Photographer's Choice/Getty Images; **8,** Digital Vision/Alamy; **10 bkgrnd,** Imagebroker/Alamy; **10 l,** Kin Images/Getty Images; **10 r,** Michael Durham/Nature Picture Library; **11,** David Pu'u/Corbis; **12–13,** Stockbyte/Getty Images; **14 l inset,** Moodboard/Corbis; **14 bkgrnd,** Chad Baker/Digital Vision/Getty Images; **15** Walter Bibikow/Danita Delimont Inc./Alamy; **16 inset,** Bettmann/Corbis; **16–17,** AP Images; **17,** Richard Megna/Fundamental Photographs, NYC; **18 bl,** Richard Megna/Fundamental Photographs, NYC; **18 b,** Richard Megna/Fundamental Photographs, NYC; **18 tr,** Nice One Productions/Corbis; **18 tl,** Matthias Kulka/Zefa/Corbis; **19 tl,** Courtesy of U.S. Army Corps of Engineers Coastal Inlets Research Program (CIRP); **19 tr,** Dorling Kindersley; **19 br,** Richard Megna/Fundamental Photographs, NYC; **19 tm,** Courtesy of US Army Corps of Engineers Coastal Inlets Research Program (CIRP); **20,** Peter Steiner/Alamy; **20–21,** Yamado Taro/The Image Bank/Getty Images; **23,** University of Washington Libraries, Special Collections, UW21414; **24 t,** David Pu'u/Corbis; **24 b,** Dorling Kindersley; **26,** Earl S. Cryer/UPI/Landov.

Interchapter Feature
Page 28, Photos 12/Alamy; **29,** Ablestock/Alamy.

Chapter 2
Pages 30–31 spread, Cheryl Gerber/AP Images; **33 tr,** Michael Clutson/Photo Researchers, Inc.; **33 tl,** Aaron Haupt/Photo Researchers, Inc.; **33 c1,** Gregory Bull/AP Images; **33 c2,** Caren Firouz/Reuters; **33 b,** Greg Baker/AP Images; **34,** Jim Reed/Science Faction; **37,** Andy King/AP Images; **38,** Harrison H. Schmitt/Johnson Space Center/NASA; **39,** Jim Byrnre/QA Photos; **35,** Ted S. Warren/AP Images; **40,** Jean Frooms/iStockphoto.com; **41 l,** Clive Barda/Arenapal; **41 r,** Gregory Bull/AP Images; **42,** Greg Baker/AP Images; **43,** Caren Firouz/Reuters; **45,** Adam Hunger/AP Images; **46 t,** iStockphoto.com; **46 bkgrnd,** iStockphoto.com; **47,** Marc Grimberg/Getty Images; **48 t,** Jorge Silva/Reuters; **48 bl,** Mark Aronoff/Santa Rosa Press Democrat/Zuma Press; **48–49 bkgrnd,** iStockphoto.com; **49,** Jorge Silva/Reuters; **50,** Clive Barda/Arenapal; **53,** AJPhoto/Photo Researchers, Inc.; **54,** Ralph Lee Hopkins/National Geographic Stock; **55,** Michael Durham/Minden Pictures; **57,** Ric Feld/AP Images; **58 t,** Ted S. Warren/AP Images; **58 b,** iStockphoto.com.

Interchapter Feature
Page 62, Jason Verschoor/iStockphoto.com; **63 t,** Chris Lemmens/iStockphoto.com; **63 b,** iStockphoto.com.

Chapter 3
Pages 64–65, Tom Barrick, Chris Clark/SGHMS/Photo Researchers, Inc.; **67 m,** Nutscode/T Service/Photo Researchers, Inc.; **67 b,** Don Carstens/Robertstock; **68 t,** Photography by Ward/Alamy; **68 bkgrnd,** J. A. Kraulis/Masterfile; **70,** Benjamin Rondel/Corbis; **71,** Clive Streeter/Dorling Kindersley; **72 l,** Mode Images Limited/Alamy; **72 bkgrnd,** Arthur S. Aubry/Photodisc/Getty Images; **74–75,** AbleStock/JupiterUnlimited/JupiterImages; **75 t,** Dave L. Ryan/Photolibrary/age Fotostock; **76 l,** Joel Sartore/National Geographic/Getty Images; **76 r,** Nutscode/T Service/Photo Researchers, Inc.; **77 t,** Goodshoot/Corbis; **77 b,** Tom Arne Hanslien/Alamy; **78 b,** Don Carstens/Robertstock; **79,** Stocktrek Images, Inc./Alamy; **80,** Brand X Pictures/JupiterImages; **82,** Image100/JupiterImages; **83 t,** AbleStock/JupiterUnlimited/JupiterImages; **83 b,** Moodboard/Corbis; **86,** Dana Hoff/Beateworks/Corbis; **88 b,** Goodshoot/Corbis; **88 t,** Clive Streeter/Dorling Kindersley; **91,** Bloomimage/Corbis.

Interchapter Feature
Page 92, Ngo Thye Aun/Shutterstock; **93,** Mark Thomas/
Photo Researchers, Inc.

Chapter 4
Pages 94–95 spread, *Cloud Gate,* Millennium Park,
Chicago (2004), Anish Kapoor. Photo © 2008 Kim Karpeles;
97 c1, Corbis/Photolibrary New York; **97 t,** Glow Images/
Photolibrary New York; **97 c2,** Dick Durrance/Woodfin
Camp; **98,** Panoramic Stock Images/National Geographic
Image Collection; **99,** Kevin Frayer/AP Images; **102 TV,**
Dmitry Kutlayev/iStockphoto.com; **102 frog,** Kitchin & Hurst/
LeesonPhoto/Digital Railroad; **103,** Glow Images/Photolibrary
New York; **105,** Alaska Stock Images/National Geographic
Image Collection; **106,** Corbis/Photolibrary New York; **109,**
age Fotostock/SuperStock; **110,** Lawrence Lawry/Photo
Researchers, Inc.; **113 tr,** Lawrence Lawry/Photo Researchers,
Inc.; **113 bkgrnd,** Norbert Wu/Science Faction; **114,** Dick
Durrance/Woodfin Camp; **119 t,** Adam Hart-Davis/Photo
Researchers, Inc.; **119 b,** Adam Hart-Davis/Photo Researchers,
Inc.; **118,** Stephen Alvarez/National Geographic Stock;
122 bl, Katherine Feng/Minden Pictures/National Geographic
Stock; **124,** John Chumack/Photo Researchers, Inc.; **125 ml,**
Edward Kinsman/Photo Researchers, Inc.; **125 mr,** Edward
Kinsman/Photo Researchers, Inc.; **125 mc,** Markus Brunner/
Imagebroker/Photolibrary New York; **128,** Richard Megna/
Fundamental Photographs; **126 l,** Adam Hart-Davis/Photo
Researchers, Inc.

Interchapter Feature
Page 130 t, Large Binocular Camera Team/AP Images;
130 b, David Steele/Large Binocular Telescope Corporation;
131 bkgrnd, JupiterImages/Creatas/Alamy.

this is your book

you can write in it

take note

this space is yours—great for drawing diagrams and making notes

this is your book

you can write in it

this is your book

you can write in it

this is your book

you can write in it

this is your book

you can write in it

this is your book

you can write in it